When The World Goes Crazy
Life's Outtakes - Year 1
52 Humorous And Inspirational Stories

By

Daris Howard

A collection of stories, humorous anecdotes, thoughts, and
tidbits of wisdom from the newspaper column
Life's Outtakes.

Publishing Inspiration

When The World Goes Crazy
Life's Outtakes - Year 1
52 Humorous And Inspirational Stories

By
Daris W. Howard

A collection of stories, humorous anecdotes, thoughts, and tidbits of wisdom from the newspaper column **Life's Outtakes**.

ISBN-13: 978-1449543518
ISBN-10: 1449543510

www.publishinginspiration.com

Publishing Inspiration

Table Of Contents

Dear Reader,

    People often ask me if my stories are true. Though I must admit that I tend to take a bit of literary license in my writing, each story is based on an actual event. Sometimes the stranger stories are the ones that are stretched the least. As people often say, truth is stranger than fiction.

    I also want to note that some of the names have been changed to protect the anonymity of the individuals.

Daris Howard

I could not have put this book together without the support of my wonderful wife, Donna. She has been and still is my editor and main support as I have written and continue to write.

I Came, I Sawed, I Conquered

✦

Trying to be a dutiful son, I help my mother when I can. So one day, when she suggested in passing that she really wanted a tree removed that was blocking her view, I made a mental note to take care of it for her. She talked about how she would like it dug clear out, so she would not have the lawn broken up. I determined I would just go out there someday and do it to surprise her.

I have to admit that I was amazed that she wanted it removed, because it did provide nice shade for the family reunions. Yet, I also had to admit that it did block the view from the window.

One day, I finally made it out there. I knew it wouldn't take me all that long. Why, it wasn't more than 12 inches in diameter. I didn't even pack a lunch.

I chose a day that I knew she would be gone visiting her brother and wouldn't be around at all. I started out by cutting the tree down. If a tree is leaning to the north, don't assume that when it's cut down that it will fall to the north. Trees have a tendency to fall in exactly the opposite direction than what you may think. I dropped it right across Mom's new picnic table. What the heck, we needed some kindling for our next cookout, and I'm perfectly fine with sitting on the ground to eat.

Next, I started digging around the roots. As I found more root, I dug wider and wider. Soon I had a hole roughly the size of a quarry - a quarry the size of Rhode Island - and I had turned the new lawn Mom had planted into a plowed hill.

I dug under and all around the roots of the tree until I thought the tree had to be loose. I found an old rusty chain and chained one end to the bumper of my pickup and one to the tree. I pulled away until the chain was tight, and then hit the gas. The chain broke and flipped forward, smashing

1

out the back window of my pickup. That ticked me off. No tree was going to get the best of me.

I found a longer, stronger tow cable, and hooked it to the tree and to my pickup. I pulled away, until the tow cable was tight, and then hit the gas; my pickup died. I tried again with the same result. I decided I needed a run at it, so I backed up and took off at high speed. There was a loud tearing of metal. I looked back and, instead of a tree out of a hole, my bumper was lying on the ground.

This was war now.

I grabbed my chain saw and started to cut through the roots. Suddenly my chainsaw bound up and died. Who would have guessed that the phone cable ran underneath one of the trees roots? I'm sure Mom would enjoy the quiet of not having her phone ring all the time, and the phone cable probably needed replacing anyway. I'm sure the waterline that I cut through did. Why, it barely broke the chain on my chainsaw. I did have to shut off the well pump and bucket out the water.

Now that my chainsaw was broken, I found a hand saw and started cutting. Soon I had every root I could find cut, but the stump would barely budge. I dug, I cut, and I dug some more, until the sweat was pouring off of me. I couldn't even take a drink of water; the well was off because the line was broken.

Eventually the tree started to move and, with a lot more coaxing and many more blisters, I finally slid it out of the hole. It was just in time, too, because Mom drove into the driveway. She walked over and, just as I expected, she was surprised. My heart swelled with pride as I announced the obvious - I had removed the tree for her.

When her shock finally subsided, she managed to speak, but they weren't the words of gratitude I'd expected. She said, "That is the wrong tree!"

A Question Of Success

The fact that I have not been successful in everything I have done in my life was brought forcefully to my attention at the Junior Miss pageant, in which my daughter was a contestant. For those unfamiliar with Junior Miss, it is a school-sponsored competition, throughout which every father feels his daughter is the obvious winner, while secretly hoping she won't win, thus sparing him the "opportunity" of hauling her all over the country to multiple events.

I have attended Junior Miss pageants many times, and have heard the whispered suggestions that the judges must have been bribed. I've laughed at the suggestion, not truly believing that anyone would bribe a judge to make sure his daughter would lose, but I suppose it could happen. I can remember the desperation mounting in my heart during intermission, as well-meaning people assured me that my daughter was surely going to win. I became increasingly sure that most of them disliked me, or they wouldn't have harassed me this way.

To satisfy the talent portion, my daughter played the harp, performing a beautiful, 87.5 second rendition of Pachebel Canon in D, leaving a whole 2.5 seconds to spare. She finished with a flamboyant pop-song surprise ending, then, instead of gliding off the stage in her flowing evening gown, the one that cost her mother two weeks of sleepless nights, she hiked it up to just below her knees, and skipped unconventionally off stage.

I breathed a sigh of relief, thinking she had lost for sure. To my amazement, the audience cheered and cheered; they loved her all the more. I knew she didn't plan to win. She had said she just wanted to have fun and hopefully win some scholarship money. She didn't have time for any of the other stuff. However, the more she did out of the norm, the more the audience adored her.

Finally, it came time for the big moment when she went to the microphone to speak her great words of wisdom. The announcer took the question she had drawn and turned to her. "How would you define success?"

She smiled at him and told how her Sweet Adeline singing group had wanted to attend a competition but had decided not to. I remembered it well. She had talked to me and told me she was afraid they would take last place. I had told her she could do worse than last. She had looked at me in surprise. "How can anyone do worse than last?"

"They could not even compete," I had answered.

In the end, they went, they competed, and they ended up near the top. As she finished the story, reciting my words with emphasis, I felt quite proud of myself for my great wisdom and my ability to influence my daughter. She finished with, "... and my Dad should know because he has attempted more things than anybody I know."

My high school friend, who was seated nearby, slapped me on the back and said, "And he has failed at all of them!" He then roared with laughter. He's that friend in high school that would always say things like he knew how I could lose 20 ugly pounds. When I would ask him how, he would say, "Cut your head off." I think he has considered it his job in life to keep me humble.

However, I couldn't help but think that he might be right this time. My filing cabinet has a drawer full of nothing but rejection letters from publishers and agents; my computer is littered with software I have developed and could not sell, books and stories I have written that I have not been able to get published, and plays that I have written that have not been produced.

Well, my daughter didn't win anything but a scholarship and the admiration of the audience.

I took her to her first summer job the other day. It was hard to see her leave home. She has been a lot of fun as a daughter, though we have had our challenges, as in any parent-child relationship. She is employed on a ranch in Jackson, driving a horse team for paying guests. My heart choked in my throat as I drove away, leaving her waving in the doorway. She now writes about the challenges she continues to face, but I'm proud to read that she still holds true to the family values we have taught her. She is growing strong in character and inner strength, just as she has grown in beauty.

I may have a drawer full of rejections, but each time I read one of her letters, I realize that maybe this old dad wasn't such a failure - after all.

Why I'm A Teacher

It was graduation day at the university where I work, and a beautiful day it was, quite unlike the first graduation I attended as a young professor. I recall that at that one, the cold south wind had swirled the snow around us.

On that day years ago, as we watched the students file past, one of my more seasoned colleagues, who was also my mentor, turned to me and said, "Graduation will be one of the happiest and one of the saddest times of your life."

When I inquired why it would the one of the saddest, he very somberly answered, "Because some of the students you have gotten to know have to leave."

When I asked him why it would also be one of the happiest, he grinned. "Because some of the students you have gotten to know have to leave."

As the procession of students ended, we marched to join them in the auditorium, filling the seats reserved for us. As the commencement droned on, my colleague reached inside the bell sleeves of his graduation robe, pulling out a book of differential equations from one and popcorn from the other. His quiet munching and flipping of pages soon drew my attention away from the redundant words which were meant to inspire.

But my colleague's words that day are etched deep into my mind. When I come across the infrequent student that is belligerent, almost daring a person to teach him, I have had to rethink why I chose to be a teacher. It obviously isn't the money. This was brought home to me some time ago, when a former computer science student of mine called me, informing me of his job at Nintendo Corporation. His starting wage was higher than my current one, though I have more education than he has, and I have worked for more than a decade. He said he knew that with my programming skills, he could get me hired, and then added, "...and the best part is, after programming, we get to play the game for six months to test it."

I thanked him, but declined his kind offer, remembering an event that had happened years earlier in a class I had taken. We were given the assignment of working on our own obituary, not as we were then, but as we hoped our life would play out. That has colored many of the decisions I have made through the years. I couldn't envision the epitaph on my headstone saying, "He loved to play games".

My mind returned to just a few days before this current graduation. While I was working on final grades, I had found a note a student had slipped in with her homework. She thanked me for being her teacher, and said the things she had learned in my class - not about math, but about life - would be things she would remember long after the math skills had faded away. As I finished reading her note, I remembered why I had become a teacher.

Now, on this sunny graduation day, as I again observed the sea of blue caps and gowns, I did so with renewed dedication and a deeper sense of satisfaction. The next semester will arrive again with its new challenges and with a new batch of eager young students, and I will, as always, be grateful I am a teacher.

As Long As I Can Carry My Own Pack

I came to the realization recently that I am no longer in my prime. The unusual part of this was that it didn't even occur at a class reunion. It happened on Labor Day. That is the day that my children think we should "labor" by hiking up Table Mountain, which overlooks the Tetons. I suggested to them that Labor Day is the day to honor women who have had children, but they didn't buy it.

This particular day was our final chance of the summer to be one with nature, away from the masses of humanity, just like the other 50,000 people who were there. We started out cheerfully singing, "...odalay, odaloe, with a knapsack on my back". The singing soon gave way to the somewhat more important task of breathing. Within a short time, my brain was asking, "Are we there yet?" and I looked back to see that we had covered almost 100 yards.

I have long since decided that, if I really want to take a 12-mile hike, I would walk from one end of a Super Wal-Mart to the other. Perhaps the "Super Wal-Mart Hike" could be a scout merit badge. Wal-Marts have drinking fountains, air-conditioning, and level floors. And, even though you have to face irate shoppers, you don't have to face mosquitoes the size of jumbo jets. Besides, I never shop the day after Thanksgiving, so the only irate shoppers I encounter are the ones from whose cart I accidentally take something, thinking it is the clearance basket.

The fact still remains that it has become an annual family tradition to hike Table Mountain. I have ten children and the youngest is still three. I don't take them until they are twelve, so I still have at least nine years of this insanity to endure. This dawned on me about two miles into the hike, when muscles, long dormant and atrophied, roared out of their slumber, attacking me. I wondered why my wife couldn't have had all ten children at the same time and saved me this grief.

Finally, reaching the last 100 yards and crawling onto the top, I looked at my feet. My blisters had blisters. In fact, I think the blisters on my feet had a five-generation family reunion.

After catching our breath, we pulled out loaves of bread and peanut butter. We had forgotten the jam. No one complained. No one cared. We were too tired to care. When we finished, there were still three loaves left. Since I was hauling the lunch, I coerced some college students into taking the leftovers.

A half hour after we arrived on top, my children were ready to start the trek down. My muscles had gone back to sleep and, as I stood up, they attacked with more venom than before. I looked down from that height, realizing I had no choice this time; turning back was not an option. That was when the over-the-hill moment hit me. My son noticed that I was walking like a duck and offered to carry my pack.

When they were small, I carried their packs and almost all of the food and water. I refused his offer. Even though I had to admit I was tired, I did make it down off of the mountain carrying my pack and my pride the whole way.

Wearily, we crawled into our van, and my children vowed they would never make that trip again. Though that was seemingly good news, my hopes didn't last long. Just like a woman in labor who swears she will never have another baby, the memory of the pain soon passed for my children, and they are already planning next year's hike.

So, if you are up on the mountain on Labor Day, watch for me. I'll be there - at least as long as I can still carry my own pack.

Uncle Hickory and the Model T

I was recently asked to make a presentation about journal writing at a genealogy conference. This got me thinking about my own genealogy, which reminded me of a saying of a famous politician. He said there is no reason to go to the work of doing your own genealogy. You could just run for political office, and then those who are opposed to you would do it for you.

However, I have, at times, found interesting stories in my own ancestral past. I noted one recently about a great uncle and a great aunt. If it hadn't been for the guilt two young men felt for what they knew was an undeserved gift from my great aunt, the story probably would have remained untold.

For anonymity, I will refer to my great aunt and great uncle as Aunt Hazel and Uncle Hickory, because some might say they were nutty. However, Uncle Hickory and Aunt Hazel were good, down-to-earth people that everyone loved. Uncle Hickory did have one well-known bad habit; he drank too much. In fact, he was fondly known as the town drunk. Everyone knew of his habit and, for the most part, tended to overlook it, due to Uncle Hickory's pleasant nature.

As one story goes, an early snowstorm struck the area the first week of October. (Imagine that here in Idaho!) Anyway, two young men, who had been hunting in the mountains, were fighting their way home through the blizzard, only to find Uncle Hickory lying snookered beside the road. Knowing they couldn't leave him there, they tossed him into the back seat of their Model-T.

Since those old cars were light, they slid all over the road, and they eventually landed in a ditch. Although the car was light, it was too heavy for one person to push out while one drove, and Uncle Hickory was too soused to be roused. The young men could get no traction, and there was nothing in the great white expanse that could be used to give the tires the grip they needed.

Finally, thinking they all would die if they didn't do something, they struck on an idea. They pulled Uncle Hickory out of the back seat and stuffed him under the tire. With the extra grab and one pushing and one driving, the car inched its way back up onto the road. Once they were finally into safe territory, and the tire had passed clear over Uncle Hickory, they carefully brushed him off and tossed him back into his seat again. Then they much more carefully headed on their way.

The young men took Uncle Hickory home and delivered him to Aunt Hazel, who put him to bed. The next day the young men received a wonderful, home-made pie with a note from Aunt Hazel. It said, "Thanks so much for giving my husband a ride home. I'm sure he would have never made it on his own. He was so stiff and sore the next morning that he could hardly walk."

Uncle Hickory's DWI

My endeavors into family history again brought me to a story of Great Uncle Hickory, the lovable town drunk. Because of his good nature, even when he couldn't remain vertical, everyone liked him. Well, everyone liked him most of the time. Uncle Hickory had one major fault when he was drunk; he liked to sing.

The quality of his voice left much to be desired, and he could never hit his pitches. Heck, he couldn't hit anybody's pitches. In fact, calling the warbling sound that emanated from his throat "singing" might be an injustice to the word, and an insult to musical people everywhere. His voice ranged from a low bass to a high, falsetto soprano, often on the same aggravating, sustained syllable. Nonetheless, what Uncle Hickory lacked in quality, he made up for in volume.

He could sing loud enough to crack windows, make the church bell vibrate, cause dogs to howl, and birds to drop out of the sky. But the biggest problem of all was that he liked to "sing" at two in the morning as he drove up and down Main Street in his old truck. This was long before the days of decibel meters and sound ordinances, and the local police were at a loss as to how they could curb his sleep-depriving revelry.

Drunken driving laws were something just barely being tested in some cities, and the desperate people of our small town took the initiative to create one of their own. Thus a remorseful, but unchanged Uncle Hickory, after one of his late night forays, found himself standing before the judge. The kind judge, who did not live in town and had therefore gotten a good night's sleep, didn't have the heart to lock up lovable Uncle Hickory. He, therefore, impounded Uncle Hickory's truck, thinking that would put an end to the problem of the late night, forte sleep-bandit and, hence, the complaints of the town's residents. Besides, he reasoned, the law was against driving drunk, and, without his old truck, Uncle Hickory couldn't drive.

However, in the early hours of the following morning, the townsfolk, much to their chagrin, heard the same dreadful braying fill the air. Uncle Hickory was dragging Main on his horse, and the horse wasn't the one doing the braying. Not long after the sun peeked over the horizon, Uncle Hickory again stood with his court-appointed lawyer to face charges brought by sleepy, irate police officers.

The judge was perplexed. The law clearly stated a person could not drive a vehicle in an inebriated state, but what did that entail? The debate raged for a period between Uncle Hickory's attorney and the prosecution as to whether a horse could be considered a vehicle. To impound one's horse was akin to horse thievery, and the judge was not about to get near that - not in the West where the memory of horse rustlers ending up on the short end of a shorter rope swinging from a tree was still recent history. With a stroke of genius, Uncle Hickory's attorney pointed out that Uncle Hickory had been too drunk to be driving.

Thus, Uncle Hickory became one of the first people, and perhaps the only person in history, to have DWI charges dropped on a technicality - having a horse as a designated driver.

Tinkertoys In My Cupboard

We have Tinkertoys in our cupboard. I'm not talking about the toy cupboard. I mean that I will sometimes pull out a bowl to put cereal in and, half asleep, pour in cornflakes and milk. I take a bite and receive 2000% of the unrecommended lifetime supply of fiber and plastic polymers. I really hate Tinkertoys in my cupboard.

"Who put the Tinkertoy in my cereal bowl?!" I holler, as I search for my missing tooth.

I really didn't need to ask that. I knew who it was. It was a 22-month-old gremlin with blond hair, blue eyes, and piggy tails. She has taken a real liking to Tinkertoys.

There are Tinkertoys in the bowls, Tinkertoys in my bed, Tinkertoys in my shoes, and Tinkertoys stuffed in the floppy drive of my computer. If I get up in the middle of the night for a drink of water, I am sure to step on a Tinkertoy and roll bruisedy, scrapity, crashity down the stairs. The last time that happened, my hollering could have put any decibel meter off the scale. I woke the whole house and most of the neighbors within a half mile radius. I swore I was going to take every Tinkertoy to the second-hand store.

But that was then. My little, blond, blue-eyed gremlin has recently been sick. We spent three days in the hospital, with her temperature soaring to 106 degrees. She slept in my arms as I comforted her, keeping her from pulling on the IV that was giving her the life-saving antibiotic. I put cool cloths on her forehead, not daring to sleep for fear she would leave me for good. I stroked her blond hair, wishing I could draw the sickness from her and take it upon myself.

At times exhaustion overcame me and I started to drift off to sleep, only to wake with a start, panicking at my lapse as I checked on her again. The three days took their toll on me as I sat in the chair, praying, with her in my arms.

Finally, her fever broke and she was able to come home. Unshaven and unkempt, I carried her from our car and tucked her gently into her bed. She still didn't want to do much and just lay there, quietly holding "bankie" close. I would come home from work each day and open the cupboard, hoping to see a Tinkertoy in my cereal bowl, but it wasn't there - none in my bed, none in my shoes, none in my computer.

Then, one day, coming in from work tired and hungry, I did pull out a plate and, to my great joy, I found a dirty, chipped, unsanitary Tinkertoy. I turned around and my little blond gremlin poked her head around the corner. Though she was still pale, her eyes had a sparkle I hadn't seen for a long time.

I held up her Tinkertoy. She came to me and hugged my knees. She then took her Tinkertoy and toddled off, humming.

You know what? I really do like Tinkertoys in my cupboard.

Halloween (In)Justice

As a faculty member at a university, I sometimes have students ask me where I live. I am leery of this, especially at Halloween time. Years ago, when I was a new faculty member, I had a colleague that enjoyed having students hit his house with toilet paper. He always felt it was a sign of their affection for him. I, personally, could do without cleaning up the mess. Thus it got so that when students asked me where I lived, I would tell them if they wanted an address I would give them one. But the address I would always give them was his. I knew this was misleading, but I didn't directly say it was mine.

Inevitably, my colleague would come to work the next day and laugh, "Those little devils hit me again!" I would just laugh along with him, especially since I was not the one who had to clean the mess out of my trees. He was surprised at the increase in his popularity in those years, and I was more than happy to let him revel in the joy of his students' love for him.

However, he grew older and eventually left us. At first I was at a loss as to what to do. But it wasn't long until a new faculty member joined our department. I nonchalantly asked him where he lived, and then memorized his address. Soon his house was getting hit by an exorbitant amount of certain squeezably soft personal paper products.

But then I made a big mistake. One Halloween, when the students asked me where I lived, I put my colleague's address on the board. I moved on with my class and forgot about it. As my lecture was ending, before I had a chance to erase the board, he walked in to prepare his class. With shock, he asked what his address was doing up there. My students looked at me and grinned, and no matter how I tried to gloss it over, I knew I was in trouble.

That particular year we owned a beautiful, female Great Pyrenees dog. We had borrowed a male Great Pyrenees to have her bred. He stood almost eye level with many people while he was standing on all fours, and when he put his paws on the fence, he looked down on almost everyone. He was especially intimidating as he protected the female, roaming diligently around our yard that nearly encompassed our house.

We heard a ruckus in the yard late on Halloween night. The male dog started going crazy. There was a loud commotion, a van door slammed, and then the van zoomed off, leaving us wondering what it was all about.

The next day, my students approached me about turning their assignments in late. They said the server that my colleague was in charge of was not working. I didn't question them further, but told them to get the assignments in as soon as possible.

Later in the day, one student came in to confess that it wasn't a server problem. He then told me that my colleague had decided to get me back. He had picked up a group of students in his van and driven to the store. He went in and bought a whole bunch of the largest packs of toilet paper they had. They had driven to my house to teach me a lesson, but had been chased off by the dog.

The student told me that when my colleague brought them back to town and dropped them off, they took all of his toilet paper with them. Then, in the early hours of the morning, when they were sure he was asleep, they went and hit his house with the toilet paper he had purchased. There was nothing wrong with the server; he knew who had done it, and he had locked their accounts.

And thus was fulfilled the scripture that says, "They shall fall into the pit which they dig for others", although my colleague might question the validity of my interpretation.

Signs of Winter

It is that time of year when I go out to help my mother winterize her yard. So recently, one evening, I took my son along to help me with the heavy lifting. I also took my two littlest girls to see their grandmother.

It was a beautiful fall day. The geese were winging their way south, honking to the rhythm of their wing beats, like a person directing the rowing of a racing canoe across the blue ocean of the sky. They were fat and happy from gleaning the grain the farmers had left behind in the yellow stubble fields.

The trees were dressed in a kaleidoscope of colors: oranges, browns, golds, and purples. The regalia they wore made them look like royalty in fine robes and golden crowns, with leaves cast at their feet, as if they were golden coins strewn in their path.

All around us the harvest was still in full swing, though it was beginning to wind down. There were plenty of potato trucks rumbling by and, no matter where a person went, the clang of diggers and pilers was audible in the autumn air. The smell of the rich dirt being rolled and tumbled by the machinery wafted across the cool breeze.

The days were already starting out crisp in the mornings, and the gardens looked like sleeping giants with quilts pulled up over their heads, as the most industrious and stubborn gardeners, reluctant to give in to the nightly frosts, tried to extend their growing season by coaxing another week or two of maturation out of their tomatoes and pumpkins.

Driving along, I nearly sent a family of racoons to racoon heaven, as they waddled out for their foray into a neighbor's corn patch. They stood on their hind legs and eyed me suspiciously, as if I might be there to steal their ill-gotten winter sustenance.

We drove along while eating hot bread that was smothered with warm apple butter, freshly made from the apple trees in our yard. The spices for pickles, cinnamon for pies, and other rich aromas of canning and baking lingered on our clothes. Our pantry was full of potatoes, apples, and carrots to enjoy through the coming winter. Jars of canned peaches, pears, applesauce and assorted jams and jellies lined the shelves.

The harvest moon hung bright and full, even though the sun was still measurably above the horizon. The clouds roiled in the western sky, carrying an ominous warning of snow in the not-too-distant future.

It was at this point that my five-year-old, Heather, turned to her three-year-old sister, Elliana, and announced that winter was coming. Elliana looked at her older sister with great admiration. "How can you tell?"

I looked at all of the beauties of the world around us, inundating our senses, and wondered which one she would expound on to explain how she knew this important fact.

She looked straight at her little sister and, in her great wisdom, said, "Because Grandma is packing up and heading south."

What To Remember When It Comes Time To Apologize

Harvest is almost over in our little community. By all indications, it went quite well, because most of the husbands and wives are still speaking to each other. There are a few that are refusing to sit on the same pew at church, but I expect that will smooth over by about December. The worst I heard of was that one husband chewed out his wife for "inattentive driving", and she left and walked back to the house until he came and profusely apologized.

This reminds me of an experience I had in the recent past. A neighbor had asked me to help him get his hay crop in. His bale wagon had broken and he needed someone to help work on the truck loading it by hand. At one point, his wife popped the clutch, tumbling hay off the back. He came flying down the piler on the side of the truck, his face beat red, and then he remembered I was there. He took a deep breath and said to his wife, "Drive more carefully!" He then climbed back on the truck, and she turned to me as I put the bales back in line, and said, "I'm glad you're here."

My neighbor's education consists of a barely squeaked out high school diploma. He is a rough looking character, with a big beard and a ragged haircut, looking much like a mountain man, and many in the community regard him as a bit of an ornery fellow. Even I have at times, though he is my friend. However, as we stepped into his small farm house for lunch, his young children were hiding and, as he came in the door, they tumbled out of their secret places, attacking him with squeals and giggles. He rolled around on the floor, playing with them, as his wife set the table. He complimented his wife on her cooking, and her love for him showed through her smile and the sparkle in her eyes.

In contrast, I went to help another man who is well educated and highly respected in the community. We worked with the few cattle he had

20

on his hobby farm. He was impatient with his children and short with his wife when she asked him when he would be ready for lunch. After we finished and we stepped into his large, beautiful house, his children hid from him in their rooms, and his wife trembled nervously when he was angry because dinner was not ready immediately. I know that sometimes when I work outside I can be impatient and hard to work with, but I hope my wife and children never fear me.

As I saw the contrast between these two men and thought about my own deficiencies, I remembered a quote from *Elbert Hubbard's Scrapbook*, "The place to take the true measure of a man is not in the darkest place or in the amen corner, not the cornfield, but by his own fireside. There he lays aside his mask and you may learn whether he is an imp or an angel, cur or King, hero or humbug. I care not what the world says of him: whether it crowns him boss or pelts him with bad eggs. I care not a copper what his reputation or his religion may be: if his babies dread his homecoming and his better half swallows her heart every time she has to ask for a five dollar bill, he is a fraud of the first water, even though he prays night and morning until he is black in the face...But if his children rush to the front door to meet him and love's sunshine illuminates the face of his wife every time she hears his footfall, you can take it for granted that he is pure, for his home is a heaven...I can forgive much in that fellow mortal who would rather make men swear than women weep; who would rather have the hate of the whole world than the contempt of his wife; who would rather call anger to the eyes of a king than fear to the face of a child."

I'm glad my wife still wants to sit on the same pew as me, but if the time comes that she leaves the truck and walks back to the house, I hope I am man enough to go apologize.

What Thanksgiving Is Truly All About

If a person is asked what they are most thankful for, nearly one-hundred percent of the time they mention family. Thus it was appropriate that, on one particular Thanksgiving, I found myself in the birthing room at a hospital, waiting for the arrival of my second child. We thought she would never come, but Thanksgiving morning found us putting our turkey back in the deep freeze, as we headed for the sterile environment of the hospital.

The smell of rolls, pies, and cranberry sauce gave way to the odors of disinfectants. The sounds of parades and football games on TV were replaced by the hum of an obnoxious monitor, broken only by intercom voices calling doctors and nurses to assignments. The nervousness I always feel when a child is born - nervousness for my wife's and my child's safety - makes me giddy, and sometimes I talk excitedly. (Actually, "I talk stupidly" is more like it.) So, as we sat watching the monitors, I started joking about how, since our little girl was going to be born on Thanksgiving, I could call her my little turkey. I joked about the different names we could name her, most of which, if mentioned here, might give me a night sleeping on the couch.

My poor wife started laughing and yelling at me at the same time, telling me that laughing during contractions made it hurt worse, and finally she took her pillow and hit me to make me stop.

When the nurse came in, the monitor had gone clear off of the chart. She was concerned until I told her I was telling my wife jokes. She was very stern with me. "Don't make her laugh," she said threateningly, "or I might just give you a taste of it yourself!" I'm not sure what she meant, but I knew by her tone that I didn't want to find out.

I don't know if it is just me, but I think labor room nurses are an interesting lot. The whole time the woman is in labor, the nurses never smile, never joke, never laugh, as if a storm cloud hangs over them. Then, once the baby arrives, it is as if the cloud lifts and they are born again, and they smile and laugh and joke and celebrate. I asked one of them about it once, and she said it is because they are all women and they feel empathy for the lady having the baby. The nurse I asked poked me in the chest and said, "You just have a baby sometime, Buster, and you'll feel the same way."

For some reason, a man in the birthing room is never the most popular person. It is like the nurses think all the grief in the world, at that moment, is his fault. I've even seen male doctors told off for an unintentional remark, like "this might hurt a little", when he should have said something like "this may hurt so much you will want to kick me through the wall".

My wife had been going to a female doctor. The doctor called the day before Thanksgiving and asked how things were going. At that point, already a week overdue, it seemed like the baby was not in a particular mood to change addresses, so the doctor went to Salt Lake to be with family. That was all it took for the baby to decide to make her grand, or should I say, prolonged, entrance onto the stage of life.

Thus we found ourselves with a doctor we didn't know, nurses that, at first, acted like either they or I had been sucking on lemons, and a noisy monitor with an attitude. But our little Thanksgiving bundle was finally born. To celebrate, the now-happy nurses brought us freezer-burned turkey, dried-out stuffing, and barely-edible cranberry sauce. But it didn't really matter, because the true meaning of Thanksgiving was locked deep in my heart, when the sweet little bundle was placed in my arms.

When The World Goes Crazy On Your Cell Phone

I think that my cell phone must have been reincarnated from a past life. I am supposedly the first owner of the given number, and yet I have received some very strange calls. Perhaps it is simply because my number is two digits in alternating sequence and easy to hit. What I do know is that the calls I have received are bizarre enough that people might feel I am making this up. I might exaggerate a little at times, but sometimes the truth is much stranger than fiction, and this is even too strange for me to make up.

Oh, I receive the usual calls from little kids who think they have punched in their dads' phone numbers, but recently the strangeness has escalated. Just last week I received a call from a lady who was mad at me before I even said hello. "Roger," she sputtered angrily, "if you think you can just dump me this way, you'll be sorry!"

"I'm sorry," I said, "but you've got the wrong number."

Her anger was evident as she responded. "Oh, you think you're so cute playing these little mind games, but you can't fool me, you big jerk."

"No, I'm serious," I told her. "You have the wrong number."

At this, she started to cry. "You are such a big liar! You don't care about anybody but yourself!"

I considered trying to ease the tension by pretending I was Roger and saying something funny like, "Hey, I'm not as big of a liar as I used to be, now that I'm on the Atkins Diet," but somehow, I didn't think she was in the mood to be teased. Besides, Roger might be roughly the size of a gorilla, so I again gently tried to tell her she had the wrong number.

"Okay!" she yelled. "Just be that way! You wait until I get hold of you!" With that, she hung up, making me feel like a real heel, and appreciative of the fact that my name wasn't Roger.

I didn't think the calls could get any stranger, but I got two incredibly weird calls a day apart. The first was from a man whose phone number indicated he was from a big city back east. He called me Jeff and, before I could say a word, he started giving me some very critical and confidential information on a big company and its internal problems. When he finally stopped to ask my advice, I was tempted to advise him to sell any stock he had, but, instead, I told him he had the wrong number.

"Aren't you, Jeff?" he asked. I told him I wasn't. "Are you sure?" he responded. I checked in the mirror and then assured him I wasn't. "Don't you work for BIG COMPANY?" he queried further. I told him I didn't. At that point, due to things that the media says goes on in board rooms, I thought he might respond, "Oh great! Now I'm going to have to kill you!" Instead, he just graciously cussed and hung up.

I thought I had pretty much received my lifetime allotment of strange phone calls, but the next afternoon, I received yet another. I looked at the number, and it was a strange, long number - very long, perhaps originating in a foreign country. When I answered it, a lady with a strong, unfamiliar accent responded, "Ello. I call about you pet rhino."

"I don't have a pet rhino," I told her.

"Then vhy you say you do?"

"I didn't say I do."

"Oh, sure, you think funny go post ad for pet rhino when you no have one."

"I didn't post an ad for a pet rhino."

"You fink I stupid or something?"

I was beginning to think that might be the first thing she got right in our whole conversation, but I didn't like the tone of the conversation or where it was heading, so I tried to inform her she had the wrong number. "Ya, right, you no fool me!" she said angrily, and hung up.

Now, every time my phone rings, I look warily at the number. I don't know a lot of things, but I do know a company whose stock I don't plan to invest in. I also know that Roger, if you're listening, you might want to skip the country. Perhaps, if you have a pet rhino, I know a number you can call and they might hide you.

Hidden Talents That Probably Should Stay Hidden

My wife says our children are going to grow up psychotic. I'm not sure why she says that. She said it once when I was expounding on a song my five-year-old, Heather, came home singing from kindergarten. "Up on the housetop, reindeer pause..."

"You know," I said to her, "reindeer don't have paws. They have hooves. Shouldn't it be, 'Up on the housetop, reindeer hooves'?"

Heather looked at me dubiously. "Daddy, the song says paws, so they have paws."

"I'm sure reindeer have hooves," I told her. For some reason, my children view things that I tell them with skepticism, even at five years old. She narrowed her eyes at me. "Have you ever seen a reindeer?"

"No," I answered.

"You see, then you don't know. And I'm sure they have paws. Besides, 'hooves' doesn't rhyme with 'Santa Claus'."

"I have seen pictures of reindeer, and they have hooves," I answered. "And perhaps it is really supposed to be Santa Clooves, and someone got it wrong."

She looked at me like I was a couple quarts short of a full eggnog. "Well," I continued. "Why don't you ask your teacher tomorrow if reindeer have hooves or paws, and then we'll know the proper way to sing it."

My wife turned to me. "You know, you might be getting another phone call from the school."

I nodded. It wouldn't be the first time a teacher wondered if I had escaped from an asylum somewhere. My innate desire to make up words to children's songs is probably why they decided I shouldn't teach nursery anymore at the church I attend. Parents would come to me and say their children came home singing songs they had never heard before. For the most part, they were the same songs, but the words were different. It is a handy habit when I get to a verse for which I can't remember the words. A friend of mine, instead of making up words, simply hums. It drives me crazy to hear him sing. "Oh give me a home where hum hum hum and antelope play hum hum hum..."

I'd rather fill in the bars. "Oh, give me a ranch, with a horse that's named Blanch, and a cow that's named Cowamazoo, a pig that's named Fred, at least till he's dead, and then we'll just call him stew. Home, home on the ranch, where the cowboys all work till they drop; where the cows all relax, as they lay on their backs, so the cream can all come to the top."

Even my wife shakes her head at me, as if she wonders whether I'm hitting on all cylinders. One day, a song from my youth came on the "Oldies" station. I hate it when the songs I sing are called "oldies", because it makes me feel, well, old. Anyway, they started singing, "Yummy, yummy, yummy, I got love in my tummy and I feel like a lovin' you..." My wife turned to me in shock. "When you sang that, I thought the words were so strange, that I was sure *you* had made it up!"

Well, if you are ever somewhere and someone is singing the wrong words, it's probably just me. Perhaps, it would be better if I just learned to hum.

The Story Of Santa's Christmas Sack

Now and then, one of my younger children will ask me how Santa fits all the toys in his sack. I tell them about a Christmas we had many years ago. It was a tough Christmas. We were a young married couple, going to college, with a brand new baby. There was hardly enough money for the necessities, like rent, let alone the luxuries, like food. Besides the tuition and the many other expenses, we were making payments to the hospital. Sometimes, gas for our vehicle could not even be purchased, and I found myself riding a bike the six miles to the university through the snow and cold, with bits of cardboard stuffed in the bottom of my shoes to help keep the water from coming through the holes in them.

Our major source of income came from any job I could find on the work board at the university, though they weren't constant nor high paying jobs. It was at this point that my wife and I made the decision that we could not afford presents. Shortly after Thanksgiving, we took my new little daughter's favorite toys and hid them so we could wrap them up for Christmas, and at least have something for her to unwrap.

Just before Christmas, I got some steady work with a carpet cleaning company. I worked hard, but every dime that came in seemed to be eaten away by past bills. The discouragement of hard classes, little money, and long hours began to settle on me like the long, dark days at the North Pole. To find my way out of this bleak time, I determined I would find some way to save some money, any money, to buy my wife something for Christmas. I tried to save tips or any little extra I could, even though I was still forced to use them at times. As I finished up my last job on Christmas Eve, just before midnight, I counted my change and barely had five dollars.

I wanted her surprise to be something Christmasy, yet it needed to be practical, so I hurried to a grocery store which closed at midnight. When I was young, the only time I got oranges or nuts was at Christmas, and I decided to buy some for her. At ten cents a pound, I bought a forty pound box of oranges, about five pounds of nuts, and had enough left over for a candy bar.

I drove home with my surprise and left them in my pickup. Our small apartment had one bedroom that wouldn't fit both a crib and a bed, so we slept on a lumpy hide-a-bed in the living room. When my wife went into the bedroom with my daughter, I raced outside and hauled the loot in and stuffed it in the coat closet.

About 2:00 in the morning, when my wife and daughter were asleep, I snuck into the bedroom to retrieve one of my wife's stockings. Now, I must say that I grew up with almost all brothers, so I knew very little about women or women's things, so, in the dark, when I reached in her drawer and pulled out a nylon, I figured it was as good a stocking as any. I stumbled my way back to the coat closet and started stuffing oranges into it as fast as I could. Every once in a while, I would reach into it to see if it was getting full, but the level of oranges never seemed to rise. At one point, my wife stirred, and I was sure she was waking, so I quickly threw in my "I Love You Coupons", which were 3X5 cards with things I had written on them like, "One I Love You Coupon Good For Breakfast In Bed" and things like that. I also threw in the nuts and the candy bar.

Her breathing leveled out so I started throwing in more oranges. But they were now noisily hitting the nuts and the cards. She sleepily asked what I was doing. "Nothing," I answered. "Go back to sleep." That doesn't work on Christmas morning, and she rolled over and turned on the lamp by her bed.

For the first time I saw her nylon - almost a full box of oranges in it - stretched wide enough you could fit all the people from a third world nation within its borders. She covered her mouth, trying not to laugh, but finally could contain herself no longer without choking, and she chortled gleefully, as I blushed in embarrassment.

And that, I tell my children, is why Santa's sack will hold all of those toys. It is made out of nylon.

My First Christmas Angel

My wife, Donna, says I have a real ability to see the humor in almost anything. I think that is because I have learned that I much prefer laughing to crying and, if I couldn't laugh at life, I'm afraid I would become very pessimistic - something I don't want to be. However, even with my desire to look at life optimistically, there still are times in life when even the most cheerful person will struggle to view something in a positive light.

In 1996, we were expecting a little girl. As any family does, we began to plan for her. We were very excited. We had picked out a name and got things ready. We had cute little jammies, a darling blanket that had little balloons and toy trains on it, and, of course, a cute little brown bear. Then, just before Christmas, my wife was concerned, because she hadn't felt the baby move for a while. She scheduled an appointment with the doctor and asked someone to come watch our children. I met her at the doctor's office to offer support, in case the worst became inevitable.

And the inevitable was what we found. Our little Tracie was gone. It was the twenty-third of December. I took Donna to the hospital and got her checked in. I went home to take care of the children, getting them dinner and readying them for bed. Then I went back to the hospital. When our little Tracie came, she was so small, yet perfect. Our hearts ached and our arms felt empty for the little baby we had already grown to love, but would never have a chance to hold. Over time, people tried to comfort us by saying they were sure, if we had to lose her, that it was good it had happened before we had loved her. I realized that those who said that meant well, but the love of a parent for a child starts long before that child is born.

Donna and I shared a quiet time together, and it was hard not to wonder what our little girl would have been like, had she come to our home. As I went home, early in the morning of December 24th, my empty arms made my heart ache. Every person deals with grief in their own way. I couldn't sleep, and finally got up and wrote a song, something I do at times when my emotions are near the surface.

*Rest well, my baby, I love you.
God in heaven loves you, too.
As you dream, His angels watch over you.
Rest well, my baby, rest well.

And when the dawn is coming,
I'll be there for you
To hold you in the morning
And love you all day through.

Rest well, my baby, I love you.
God in heaven loves you, too.
As you dream, His angels watch over you.
Rest well, my baby, rest well.

And God will love and keep you.
You're His baby, too.
And I'll be there to greet you,
When dawn brings life anew.

Rest well, my baby, I love you.
God in heaven loves you, too.
As you dream, His angels watch over you.
Rest well, my baby, rest well.

And thus, my first Christmas Angel joined Jesus to celebrate His birthday, on the day when the Christian world is filled with the hope given by the birth of another child, many centuries ago.

The music to this can be heard at:

http://www.darishoward.com/music.php

A Rising Star On The Theatre Stage

During this time of year, my family is often asked to do Christmas programs for different groups. Sometimes we will be asked to do a program for the nursing home. Other times we might be asked to prepare a program for a community dinner. Since I am much more limited in talent than my wife and my children, I am usually the master of ceremonies. I prepare the regular jokes that no one laughs at, and stories that put people to sleep. The rest of my family prepares the music.

Inevitably, I am also in charge of trying to encourage the little ones to do their parts. When my little Heather was three, we dressed her up in a doggy costume. Her six year old sister, Clarissa, was going to sing, "How much is that doggy in the window?" at which point Heather was going to bark like a dog. We had practiced it and practiced it, encouraging Heather with a bribe of candy. It was a really cute act and she had it down well.

Then came the day of the performance. As we practiced back stage, Heather balked. "I don't want do doggy," she said. "I want do kitty." I told her we had to do it just like we practiced. We started the practice. "How much is that doggy in the window?" Clarissa sang. Heather followed with "Meow, Meow". We stopped. "Now look!" I said to Heather. "We practiced doggy, you are dressed like a doggy, the program says doggy, you've got to do doggy!"

We started again and Clarissa sang, "How much is that doggy in the window?" and Heather stubbornly said, "Meow, meow." We stopped. I took a deep breath. "Ok, Heather," I said, "you do kitty if you want, but I don't give candy to little girls that do kitty."

It was too late to try to bribe her further; she was on. I didn't know how it was going to turn out. With children, you often don't. They got into position, and their mother played the introduction. Then Clarissa sang, "How much is that doggy in the window?" Their mother paused. Heather slowly looked to the side of the stage where I stood. Then, with absolutely no expression, and as monotone as she could, she said, "Woof....Woof."

Heather never did have stage fright. She could get in front of an audience from the time she was small. Her problem was that she didn't see the sense of it. I could bribe her with candy, but the minute the candy was gone, she was off the stage. To try to keep her on the stage, I learned to give her hardtack candy she couldn't chew, but had to suck on.

However, that all changed one summer as she watched us perform a melodrama. She was almost four by then, and she was supposed to stay in the concession stand with her brothers and sisters. Instead, she got her little bag of popcorn and staked out her seat on the front row. She watched every performance, mesmerized by the action on stage. From that moment on, something clicked with her. I didn't realize how much until the next play. She had a part with a stage name of Hannah. One day I was trying to get her to move across stage. I said, "Heather, we need you to move." She didn't respond. After a few attempts, I finally went on stage and took her hand. "Heather," I asked, "why don't you pay attention to me when I'm talking to you?"

"Because," she answered, "my name isn't Heather; it's Hannah." From that point on, she would never respond to the name 'Heather' on stage, but only 'Hannah', and I knew a little actress was born.

New Year Resolutions

It's that time of year when all of my friends are making their New Year resolutions. Most of them are ridiculous and totally unreasonable, like never falling asleep in church, or reading the whole book of *Gone With The Wind* in under 12 months. As for me, I am more of a realist. I like to choose goals that I am sure I can obtain.

"Honey," I commented to my wife, as I was listing my New Year goals, "I think I will not smoke or drink this year."

"But you don't smoke or drink, now," she replied.

"I know that," I told her.

But there is another goal that I have decided I must take on - one that I know will tax my limited abilities. My determination is fixed and my resolve is set.

It all started back when my wife and I were asked to co-direct a community theatre production. We went to meet with the other husband-wife team, with whom we would be working, whom I will call John and Mary. We had finished tryouts and had the regular people show up. Most of the parts were filled, but we still had a lead male adult role we could not find a person for.

We decided we would look at the tape from the production the year before and see if there was anyone we could coerce into joining our cast. That production the year before had been my first experience with theater. I, myself, had been coerced into making a fool of myself on stage in front of thousands of people, instead of the way I normally do it in life - in front of a few people at a time.

Anyway, we started watching the tape. As I marched onto stage on the video, making my debut performance, Mary became excited.

"How about him?!" she exclaimed. "How about that short, fat

guy?!'"

John almost choked. "What did you say?"

"I said, 'how about that short, fat...'"

John cut her off. "Yes, I heard what you said. Do you know who that is?"

She shook her head. John coughed and nodded his head slightly in my direction. Suddenly, Mary caught what he was trying to tell her. She looked at me, then back at the video and then at me again. Her face flamed bright red, outlined by her blond hair, and she took on the appearance of a dim neon light bulb.

She spoke hoarsely. "It's not that I am saying you are fat, or anything. No, it's just that you do a good job playing a fat guy."

John coughed and choked.

"What I meant to say is that you cover up well how fat you are when you..."

John didn't even let her finish this sentence before he started choking and gasping like he needed a ventilator.

"What I really was inferring was..." Mary paused, and I could see in her expression that her mind was whirling as the video continued to play. "What I really wanted to say was, 'Would anyone like some cookies?'"

With that, she fled from the room before anyone could even answer. Shortly, she came back with some warm chocolate chip cookies. She offered them to each of us. I know at that point the proper thing for me to have said was, "No thanks, I'm on a diet," but what I really wanted to say was, "I'm not really hungry, so I'll just take five or six."

Anyway, that steeled my resolve, and I finally realized I had to buckle down and make a tough New Year's resolution.

I'm sure you've guessed it. I've finally decided I need to get more fat friends so they will help me look thinner.

Things I Resolve To Do Before It's Too Late

✦

I sat holding a beautiful scarf - a Christmas present from many years ago. The magnificence of its interwoven patterns of red and black was particularly amazing because the woman who had knitted it for me was blind.

Many years ago, as a young man of twenty, I was living far from home in New York at Christmas time. Many of the good people from the church I attended helped eased my homesickness. None did so more than Norma.

She was like a mother to me. She often invited me over for dinner after church and treated me like a son. Her home was an interesting study in efficiency, especially with her lack of vision. Her deceased husband had also been blind and, unable to have any children of their own, they had adopted handicapped children that no one else would accept.

Each physically handicapped child was paired with a mentally challenged sibling. Together the two became a team - the mentally capable child directing the actions of his or her physically capable brother or sister. There were eight children when I was there.

The love that emanated from these children filled the home with a peacefulness that I have seldom felt anywhere else. I would often have a child slip their hand into mine and express their love for me, never fearing that expression, as many of us do.

As time went on, Norma remarried a good man named Bill, and my life took me far away. But at Christmas time, my heart often followed memories back to that humble home. Life overwhelmed me, at times, and I didn't keep in touch as well as I should have.

Then, one day in 1998, I received a phone call. The woman said I didn't know her, but she was trying to contact a young man who had grown up in the vicinity of Ricks College. She said she had been in touch with a college student there, and had asked her for a phone number of someone with the last name of Howard. The young woman had given her my name, for I was the only such faculty member at the time.

The woman asked me if I might have a relative that had lived in Rochester, New York, in about 1982. By the time she finished the explanation, I had recognized her voice. I said "Norma, it's me." I had no sooner said her name than she started to cry.

We had a long, happy visit. It was so good to talk to her again and to find out about each of her children. As I vowed I would keep in contact with her, she was very quiet. I sent a Christmas letter every year after that, but I didn't hear any more from her. So this year I decided to call.

I called just after Thanksgiving, and a lady with a southern accent answered. I asked for Norma, and she said, "Norma has been daid 8 years, and I'm now Bill's wife."

I was shocked, for I had never been told. She gave the phone to Bill. He told me that Norma died in August of 1998. I learned that she had been diagnosed with cancer, and knew she had very little time left when she had called me, but had chosen not to reveal it.

My heart ached, and yet, I was happy to know that when she knew she was approaching her final days, she had taken the time to contact me for one last visit. As I hung up the phone, I was overcome with emotion. I picked up the beautiful scarf and wrapped it around me. The warmth it gave me came more from the memories it brought than the cold it kept out, for I felt as if Norma herself had wrapped her arms around me to express her love once again, as she had on that Christmas in 1982.

With that feeling of love came my New Year's resolution that I, too, would find those friends who left an indelible mark on my heart, before that opportunity was lost forever.

Snow and Ice

✦

I have decided that I am sick of snow and ice. It came to me all of a sudden, one morning, on my way to work. I was driving down the highway, heading south, minding my own business, when, all of a sudden, my pickup truck hit ice and decided it wanted to go home. I used to have a horse like that. Slacken the reign for one second, and she was headed back to her pasture at full speed, with or without her rider. Anyway, when I hit the ice, the horizon zipped around a few times, and I found myself heading north on the same road.

No problem, I thought. Just act nonchalant about the whole thing. I just smiled and waved at people as they went by. They waved back. However, they didn't smile, and they were only waving with one finger. I then remembered I was on a divided highway. Just stay calm, I said to myself. No need to worry about the semi truck bearing down on me in the passing lane. He's got plenty of room to stop.

He was able to get into the other lane just in time to avoid making sheet metal out of my little Toyota pickup. It must have confused him, too, because he called me a few things that didn't even come close to my real name.

So there I was, realizing that I am really getting sick of the snow. It wasn't the first time that week, either. Earlier I had decided it would be good to get some exercise. Why not go jogging? By the time I got all bundled up to go outside, I couldn't even walk, let alone jog.

My wife suggested a stationary bike. I've always felt a stationary bike was an oxymoron - you know, like "smart bureaucrat". I found one in the paper for a good price. (A stationary bike, I mean, not a smart bureaucrat.) My wife and I both agreed to work out on the bike, so we went to see it together. It was a nice one, worth a lot more than the $49.99 they were asking for it.

While my wife was writing the check, I turned to the owner, who was helping me load it. "Why are you selling it for only $49.99, if you don't mind me asking?"

"Well," he replied, "if it's under $50, then you can list it for free in the newspaper. I just wanted to get rid of the darn thing."

"Why?" I queried further.

"Because I'm sick of snow. I'm not going to ride that thing one more minute. Furthermore, I'm going to tie a snow shovel to the front of my pickup truck and drive down the road heading south. When I stop somewhere and someone asks me what that thing is tied to the front of my truck, I'm going to buy a home there and stay the rest of my life."

That was a few weeks ago. Poor guy had spring fever really bad. Somehow, the image of him in his truck heading south, with a snow shovel tied to the front, was all I could envision in my mind as the horizon spun by.

So, if you see a Toyota pickup truck with a snow blower tied to the front, just honk and wave and, if you don't wave with just one finger, I will probably wave back.

An Incredible Sale

I just saw the most incredible sale! It was totally unbelievable! I'm sure you won't believe me, but it was true. The flashing sign of a local drug store is advertising bread at "•99 cents a loaf". Wow! What a door crasher that must be! Point 99 cents a loaf. Bread for under a penny. I bet they were sold out within minutes of opening. Why, I haven't seen bread at that price since... Come to think of it, I've never seen bread at that price. Most bread I've seen costs around a dollar, when it is on sale.

My father talked about prices like that during the depression, but this is the 21st century. I was thinking I might take a dollar in there and get a hundred loaves and tell them to keep the change. I considered getting one and trying to frame it somehow. That way, when an old timer started to tell me what it was like in the good old days, I could point to the plaque of bread on my wall and say, "Yeah, well, I remember when a person could get bread for less than a penny."

But the other day, I saw an even better sale on squash. It was at "•10 cents per pound". That means, for a penny, I could get ten pounds of squash. Squash is all right, but what would I do with ten pounds of it, and if I bought less, how would they give me change? Unless... That does give me an idea. One of my neighbors stuffed my car so full of squash while I was at church last summer that I had to walk home, since there was no room to drive. It could be payback time. For ten dollars, I could get five ton of squash and fill his whole garage.

My wife thinks I am hallucinating, and my mathematician brain is working overtime. I just like to look at things logically, especially when it comes to numbers. She says that is not what they mean, but I'm sure, with the truth in advertising laws, they are just having incredible sales.

I try to watch carefully for these kind of bargains. Opportunities like this don't come around often, though I must admit, I see more of them than I would suspect. Why, I saw in an ad that a bank was now giving 110 percent. What a return that is! My wife said it only meant their service, but I informed her that a person can't give more than everything, or it would not have been everything in the first place. With that explanation, I informed her that it has to be an interest rate. What else could it be? After all, they are in the banking business, and they know numbers, so surely they know what 100 percent means.

Then there was a local store that had a 150% off sale. That was one of the best. I was going to walk into the store and tell them I wanted everything they had, and they could just write me a check for the extra 50%.

She just shakes her head at me, and refuses to let me anywhere near those great sales. Maybe she thinks I will embarrass her.

Well, I've got to wrap this up. I just noticed that the local grocery store has a sign that says its boxes of hot chocolate are ".99 cents". I love hot chocolate, and I have ten dollars in my pocket. I think I'll go buy a thousand of them.

Winter Time Gardening

It was just after Christmas, and the temperature was below zero outside, the snow covered the ground two feet deep, and my little four-year old daughter, Heather, was putting on her coat to venture outdoors.

"What are you doing?" I asked.

"I am going out to pick strawberries," she informed me.

I told her there wouldn't be any strawberries this time of year. "Have you been out to check?" she asked, skeptical of my knowledge on such matters.

"Well, no," I had to admit. "Not recently."

"Then," she said triumphantly, "maybe there are, and you just don't know."

There was no talking her out of it, so I put on my own coat, and we trudged out, mitten in hand, to check. I thought for sure, once we got to the strawberry patch and she saw the snow piled high across it, that she would realize I was right. But she was undaunted, as she was sure there were strawberries growing underneath the snow. Nothing was going to convince her otherwise, except seeing for herself. So I retrieved a shovel and started to dig. We dug down to the plants, brown in their dormant state, and still she remained unconvinced. She was sure we had just dug in the wrong place.

I think we had to uncover about half of the patch before she considered I might be right, but only maybe; she still thought I might be digging in the wrong spots. By the time we finished, our neighbors were staring out their windows at us, wondering about such things as sugar sap, and pine sap, and especially about a sappy neighbor that would drag his daughter out to dig holes in the garden in the middle of winter.

Just when I thought we were done and she would be ready to head back into the warm house, she stuck her hand into her coat pocket and

45

pulled out a mitten full of corn. It wasn't seed corn, but canned corn she had saved from dinner. She wanted to plant it. By this time my heart ached for my daughter who so loved to garden. She is so much like me, and the winter seemed so long to her.

I tried to explain to her that cooked corn wouldn't grow anywhere, let alone out in this cold. I could see tears glisten in the corners of her eyes. My mind whirred as to how I could get out of this, without hurting my little daughter's feelings. She so badly wanted to plant her corn right away. Suddenly, I had an idea. I told her I had a big pot which we would fill with dirt and put it in a south window. Together, we rummaged through the garden shed until we found the biggest planting pot we had. I dug the snow away in the garden and chiseled some frozen dirt out of it.

She impatiently checked the pot in the window off and on all day to see when the dirt would be warm enough to plant. I tried to explain again that cooked corn would not grow, but she insisted otherwise, so we planted it. After tucking her in bed that night, I found some leftover garden seed from the previous year, and secretly planted it in her pot. She checked it every day, and when the time finally arrived that the little shoots sprang from the soil, she was dragging me over to see.

A short time later, in early February, snow still thick on the ground, I found her again pulling on her coat and mittens. When I asked her where she was going, she said she was going to check the strawberries again.

"I thought I explained that strawberries won't grow in the winter," I said.

"Yes," she answered, "but you also said cooked corn wouldn't grow, and look at my plants." I looked at her plants, now about 6 inches high, and shook my head as I reluctantly slipped on my coat.

The Incredible Tale

✦

February is scout month, and I can never think of that without recalling the time I spent as scoutmaster to 18 boys. I remember that at one campout, the boys came in to the campfire dragging something. "Look what we found!" they exclaimed.

It was a big cement post with a bronze marker on it. Brushing away the dirt, I read the inscription. "Government marker. Do not remove."

"Where did you get this?" I asked.

"Oh, can you believe somebody just left it half buried in the woods?" they answered.

I insisted that we put it back, but they thought they ought to take it home and put it in the scout closet. That way they could show it off to everyone else. I could just imagine what the scout committee would say when they saw it there, that is, if they could see it among all of the other junk. I couldn't convince the boys it belonged to the government, no matter what it said, but I also obviously couldn't let them take it home. I had another idea.

"Have you guys ever thought that maybe it was left by aliens and that by pulling it out you have launched a space ship to this very spot to pick up specimens to take back to their planet?"

Now I had their attention. They might not believe it was a government marker, but an alien one was totally plausible. I suggested we put it back and watch. We carried it back to where they said they found it. We carefully slid it into its hole and put the dirt around it. The boys set up watch. I told them I would be happy to take care of camp. I returned and stretched out on my sleeping bag to catch a nap. Actually, calling it a sleeping bag is a misnomer. A person never really sleeps in one, unless he has hiked all day and is so tired he can sleep on top of a cactus. What a person really does is lay there until he gets so stiff he can't move.

By nighttime, there still weren't any aliens. "Hey, give them time," I said. "They might live a few thousand light years away. They might not get here until tomorrow."

"Yeah," one of the boys chimed in. "They might be driving a Chevy space ship, in which case they could be a lot longer than that."

"Or," retorted another boy, "They might be driving a Ford, in which case they're probably broke down out in the middle of nowhere." I thought it might not be a good idea at that point to mention that I drive a Toyota.

I decided to ease their minds by telling them a ghost story. They gathered around the fire and I began. "Once, quite some time ago, there lived in these parts a beautiful young girl of about 12 years old, who liked to wander in the forest. Then, one day, she found what was described as a pillar. When she touched it, a bright light suddenly appeared. It could be seen for miles around. When people arrived at the spot, the light was gone, and so was the girl. However, there was a dark circle burned in the grass. About a week later, an old woman of about 80 appeared and claimed to be the girl. She said she had lived on a far off planet for decades, but had somehow escaped and returned through a time warp."

Far in the distance, interrupting my story, we heard a mountain lion scream - what perfect timing! I seized on the opportunity as I continued. "Sometimes, when the moon is just right, you can hear her cry. She isn't quite human, and can never die, and she knows that someday they will return for her. So she wanders the woods, waiting to catch someone she can send in her place."

Again, the mountain lion screamed. "What was that?!" one of the boys said, jumping to his feet.

"That," said another boy, rolling his eyes, "was a whole bunch of poppycock."

"I really got to go," one of the boys said. "Who would like to go with me?"

No one else seemed to have to, though some were squirming. I asked him why he didn't just go by himself. He told me he didn't have a flashlight. I tossed him mine. He went barely out of sight. Suddenly we heard some noise behind the tent.

"Hey!" someone yelled. "That's my tent! You better not be doing what I think you're doing!"

He almost instantly returned with a relieved smile on his face.

"Well," I said, "it's about time we put out the fire and head to bed."

They reluctantly agreed. I climbed into my tent. I didn't sleep too well, though, and it wasn't just the sleeping bag, either. It's hard to sleep when everyone in the other tents refuse to turn their flashlights off.

Gender Differences On Romance

Men and women are different. I know you may not think so, but they are; they really are. I could expound on the differences, but since it is Valentine's season, when romance is measured out to us in unhealthy overdoses, I will stick to that area. In particular, I have noticed a great difference in what my wife and I view as a romantic gift.

Valentine's Day was approaching at a high rate of speed, like a Semi of love bearing down on me, a poor, unromantic Yugo. It was portending to hit me, leaving me as a small smudge of road kill on the romantic highway of life. I knew I had to come up with some kind of gift for my wife, but I was clueless about what to get.

Now, I swear that in our kitchen our appliances have personalities. Our toaster is no different. It has a dial to determine how long it traps something within its jaws, but the dial only seems to have two settings: raw and charcoal. Either you can turn it to the left, in which case it tries to throw anything back at you the second you attempt to toast it, or, you can turn it to the right, and it will lock the item deep within its teeth, growling at you if you try to rescue your food from its grasp, until all of the fire alarms in the house are screaming.

The toaster's temperament might partially be due to the things it has been fed. My two littlest girls like to try to "flush" (their word, not mine) everything they can think of down its throat, including puzzle pieces, Tinkertoys, and crayons. Even one of my older daughters has learned how to make a s'more in the toaster, something that is meant to be cooked over a campfire where, when it catches fire, it can be buried.

One day, when our smoke alarm started howling, I was not surprised, when I came into the kitchen, to find my wife wrestling the toaster for what looked like a lump of coal.

"Give it up," I said. "It isn't going to let you have it until it's had its fill."

She shook her head. "I definitely need a new toaster."

"Why?" I asked. "Don't you like pretending your bagels are all chocolate coated?"

Then, in an instant, inspiration struck, and I knew the perfect Valentine's Day gift.

And thus it was, on Valentine's Day, my family gathered around to see the thoughtful gift I had purchased. When my wife opened her new, four-slot toaster, instead of the excitement I had expected, she looked at me with her big blue eyes, lip quivering. "It's sure a nice toaster," she said, and all of my older daughters rolled their eyes in disgust.

We've been married long enough that I now can interpret the wife language quite well, though I am not fluent at speaking it, and I knew very well what she was meaning was, "You are absolutely a clueless male that got something for the kitchen and not for me!" But she was too kind to say it in English.

That's the thing we differ on. If I need a new drill or hammer to work on a project, and my birthday is coming up, I try to tell her so she can get it. Instead, I will get a tie, cuff links, a new shirt, or cologne - something that is totally useless for the project I am currently involved in.

Anyway, I think I'm getting this present thing all figured out. I have an anniversary coming up, and I know just the thing I will buy. She loves a nice, neat yard, so I will buy her a new lawnmower. Surely she will love that, especially if it is self-propelled with an electric start.

When David Takes On Goliath

When February rolls around, that month when wrestling and basketball are coming to a close, I often find my mind slipping back to my athletic days. While wrestling at the small junior college named Ricks, our coach always liked to start off the season by taking us to the Boise State Invitational. The other competitors at the tournament were all four year universities, including wrestling powerhouses like B.Y.U., U.C.L.A., and others. I think he did this to humble us and help us see how far we had to go. If that was his purpose, it was very effective.

One match in particular that I remember was not even my own, but that of the heavy-weights. Boise State had a heavy-weight wrestler that was approximately the size of a draft horse. He stood nearly seven feet tall. The story was told that when they tried to get an official weight on him, they couldn't do it with any scale at the university, since those topped out at 500 pounds. They ended up taking him down to the local grain elevator and weighing him on the truck scale.

I don't know if the story was true or not, but I do know that a person couldn't realize how big he was until they stood next to him and stared eye-level at his belt buckle. Everything about him was large. His hands were about the size of a Volkswagen, and his feet were not a foot, but a yard. He breezed through the tournament, pinning every opponent in the first round.

Another highly ranked heavy-weight was from B.Y.U. He was only 190 pounds, but what he lacked in weight he made up for in speed and agility, and he was powerfully strong.

As was expected, the two faced off for the championship. The excitement that was built for the match was palpable. Speed and agility facing enormity. It was billed as a David and Goliath rendevous. The time for the match finally arrived, and the gym was packed, as everyone waited anxiously for the starting whistle of a match that was sure to be memorable.

The two opponents lined up across from each other and shook hands. And then the whistle blew. In a blur, B.Y.U. shot in with a beautiful attack. And that was as far as it went. He heaved and strained and pushed, but Boise didn't move.

It reminded me of a show called **Bambi vs. Godzilla**. It starts out with Bambi grazing peacefully in the forest, looking up once in a while, as the birds chatter happily. Suddenly, out of nowhere, a giant reptile foot appears, descending from above Bambi. The next shot shows a flat deer. Roll the credits; the show is over. The whole reel was probably less than 60 seconds long.

Anyway, after B.Y.U. had tried for some time to move Boise, with no success, Boise reached his big bear paws down and stuck them around B.Y.U.'s middle, touching fingertip to fingertip. Then he peeled B.Y.U. off from himself, gently turned him over, laid him on the mat, and dropped on him with all the subtlety of an earthquake.

All that could be seen sticking out from under Boise were two wrestling shoes. There they stayed for some time while the ref was trying to get into a position to determine the results. Finally, Boise, annoyed at the delay, in his big booming voice said, "Ref, he's pinned."

The ref, bothered that someone should tell him his job, replied, "No, he's not!"

That was when we heard a muffled voice, as if gasping for air. "Yes, I am! For cryin' out loud! Get him off me! Get him off me!"

And thus ended the David and Goliath story. But in this story, I learned an important lesson. Goliath not only often wins, but usually annihilates David.

Do You See Signs Of Aging?

$\dagger$

"Do you see signs of aging?" the advertisement asked. I looked in the mirror. "Me?" I laughed. "Never!"

In preparing to go on a trip to Peru, I started searching through all of my old stuff to find a birth certificate for a passport. I came across my high school senior picture. I laid it aside as I continued my search. One of my teenage children came wandering into the room and picked it up. She looked at it - it showing my state wrestling champion build - and then she looked incredulously at me. "Is this you?" I smiled and nodded. She looked at the picture once more, and then at me again, and, with shock in her voice, asked, "What happened?"

Upon finding my birth certificate, I took it with me so I could stop by the post office later in the day to get my passport application finished. I drove my children to school while listening to the radio. The announcer told us that he was going to play a "golden oldie". The radio started softly playing, "...how deep is your love...". I was humming along, remembering that it had been the theme song for my Junior Prom, when one of my children said, "Can you believe what they sang fifty years ago? And what a pathetic name, 'Muskrat Love'."

The day wore on, and I needed to pick up my ten-year-old daughter from the middle school. I ran into an acquaintance there and we visited. As my daughter and I turned to leave, the woman looked at my daughter, then said to me, "It's nice to see grandfathers like you that are so involved in the lives of their grandchildren."

My family does a lot of theater, and we had a dress rehearsal for one of our plays. My daughter is always kind about doing my makeup since, when I put it on, it looks as if I was trying to adhere it to my face with a four inch brush in the back seat of a car while driving over a washboard road. As she gently applied the make-up, she said, "I like doing your makeup, Dad, because I can easily see your age lines to draw them in." I took a deep breath, swallowing my pride, and she scolded me. "Don't frown so much! It makes them too deep, and I draw them too dark."

I finally got to the post office to do my passport. The official looked at my birth certificate. "We can't use this; it's too old. You need a modern one with the appropriate seal." She was just handing it back, when she glanced at it again. "Besides, I think the date on it is wrong. According to this, you'd only be in your forties."

As I was putting my memorabilia away, I came across a picture from our wedding day. "Is that Momma?" my five year old, Heather, asked. I told her the woman in the picture was indeed her mother. "She's pretty!" she exclaimed. She then called her three-year-old sister over. "Look, Elli, Momma was a princess."

I smiled at their delight in discovering how pretty their mother was on our wedding day. Then, Heather turned back to me and asked, "Who's the guy with her?"

I told her it was me. She looked at me incredulously, then back at the picture, again at me, then back at the picture, then she laughed, unable to believe what I was telling her. "Oh, Daddy, you're so funny!"

I saw the ad from the magazine, and looked at it one more time. "Do you see signs of aging?" I glanced at the two pictures, my senior picture and my wedding picture. "Well," I thought to myself. "Maybe just a little."

The Real March Madness

March Madness always reminds me of the time my daughter, Trissa, who was six, asked me if she could play youth basketball.   In my state of innocence, I could see no reason she shouldn't. I drove her down to the city building to sign up. Outside, I saw some dads sitting in their cars. They would tell their daughters to go in and find out how much it cost, and bring the papers back out for them to sign.

"What a bunch of couch potatoes," I thought, assuming it was just a matter of laziness. "Why don't they get off their duffs and just go in with their daughters?" I went in and found mostly girls, with a few moms. When we worked our way up the line, and were finally standing at the sign up table, the lady looked over her glasses and carefully sized me up. I realize now I must have had some invisible sign hanging on me that said "Sucker".

"Have you ever thought about coaching one of these teams?" she asked.

I honestly had never thought about coaching any team, let alone one made up of small girls. I told her I hadn't played team basketball since high school.

"Oh, it's no problem," she said. "With girls this age, all you have to do is teach the fundamentals. You know, dribbling, shooting - that kind of stuff."

"Well," I stammered, pausing to look at all the young girls around me. "I'm not sure."

"I'm positive it wouldn't be a problem for someone of your athletic ability," she quickly added.

I looked down at my potbelly, and wondered how she knew inside that marshmallow body of mine was a former athlete screaming to get out - or perhaps just screaming. But she had me, and she knew it. I signed my name to the line that said "coach", and she told me how I could get hold of a key to a gym where we could practice two days a week.

Within two days, she had called me with the list of eight girls, all six to seven years old, that were to be on my team. My daughter was, of course, one of them. I decided to take her outside and get started before our first practice. I mean, the coach's daughter should have every advantage. We went out and I showed her how to dribble and do a lay up.

She started bouncing the ball and took off toward the basket. The ball continued bouncing where it was, and she ran to the basket, jumping into the air with no ball in hand.

"Well, at least her form was good," I thought.

I decided I needed to just teach her how to dribble the ball. I dribbled the ball in place for a minute, and then told her to try. On the first bounce, it ricocheted off of her shoe and bounced down the driveway. We tried again, with her concentrating carefully. She got a few bounces out of it, but it got lower and lower, and she had to pick it up and start again. It reminded me of myself trying to do a yo-yo.

Anyway, after about an hour of this, I decided she must have inherited her basketball skills from her mother, along with her beauty and musical talent, and I decided to call it a day. I felt it was my fault for not having worked with her sooner, but I was glad the other girls would have better skills.

Practice finally came. I asked each girl a little about themselves.

Only one girl, Kathy, had ever played before. She had all brothers. The rest weren't even sure what the purpose of the game was. "Can I be the quarterback?" Ellen asked.

Another little girl named Shara, snickered. Shara was the wiriest of the girls and had long black hair, a short fuse, and an almost y-chromosome. "There aren't any quarterbacks in basketball, Stupid," Shara said to Ellen. "You either have to be a front, a back, or a middle."

"Close," I said. "It's forward, guard, or center."

"That's what I said," Shara snipped at me, and then lashed out with her foot, catching me hard in the shin.

And that's where the madness came in, as I knew immediately it was going to be long season.

A Basketball Coach's Dilemma

It was the first practice with my basketball team, which consisted of eight girls that were six and seven years old. Every girl received a basketball with her fee, so we started practice by dribbling in place. Laura, who had already lost her basketball, showed up with a tennis ball instead.

Basketballs were rolling everywhere. Only two girls could bounce the ball halfway straight: Kathy, the most experienced girl, and Laura with her tennis ball. Finally I stopped the chaos. I had them all put the balls away, except for Laura, and we practiced dribbling the tennis ball. It took a while, but they were finally getting it straight up and down. I was just thinking we were making some progress when we had a major catastrophe - Leslie broke a finger nail. She showed me her hand as big tears poured down her face. I was shocked to see that all of her other finger nails were about the size of railroad spikes. "Why don't you just trim the rest to match?" I suggested.

She looked at me with great disdain and disbelief. "Are you crazy?! You know how long it took me to grow these?! My mom is going to be so, so, so mad about this!" She sniffled a minute, and then she glared at me. "You are in such big trouble!"

Next, we tried to dribble from one end of the court to the other. I was in the process of dividing them into two teams for a relay, when Leslie complained. "But what if we get sweaty? If I get sweaty, I lose the curl in my hair, and it's so totally gross." I looked at Leslie, who could pass as a Munchkin Miss America, and just shook my head.

Shara, who never worried about anything feminine, demanded, "I want to be on the opposite team from Leslie."

I finally had the teams formed, and all of the girls, with the exception of Kathy, would take off down the court, and within a couple of steps, they outran the ball, leaving it far behind. Kathy was able to dribble the length of the court, but she was a bit out of shape - in fact, she was a lot out of shape. Once she got to the opposite end, she would have to sit down and rest for a couple of minutes before she could dribble back.

It took more than two weeks before most of the girls could dribble the length of the court. The first game was approaching and I hadn't even taught them how to shoot. I decided that would be the topic for our next practice.

I had the girls line up in front of the basket. The first girl threw the ball into the air with both hands, using an underhand throw. It went straight up and came down on her head. That took her out of play for half the season. The next girl threw the ball as hard as she could, and it didn't even hit the bottom of the net. With the exception of Kathy, no one even came close to the rim. Kathy could sometimes make a basket, if she was not flustered, if she was given about three hours to stare at the basket, if the wind was blowing just right, and if the stars were all aligned and the cosmos was happy. I was desperately thinking of suggesting to the youth league that we let the girls play basketball with tennis balls and lower the basketball rim to five feet, but I thought for sure they would laugh at me.

I was also sure that every other coach had teams that could dribble and shoot. I had never seen a young girls' basketball team play, but I knew I must be the world's biggest failure as a coach, and, as the day of their first game approached, I wondered what I had gotten myself into. I could just imagine a score of 40 to 0, or something like that, because a team can't score points if they can't even hit the basket.

But, like it or not, game day came, and, though I wanted to pretend I was sick, I knew I needed to be there with my team, especially if Leslie broke another finger nail.

Young Girls, Basketball Games, And Chaos

✦

The day of our first game finally arrived for my basketball team of six and seven year old girls. I was sure we were going to look foolish, as bad as they were, but as we went out to warm up, I could see the girls on the other end of the floor bouncing basketballs off of their feet, and shooting and not even hitting the net, and I felt much better.

The ref called for a girl from each team to come to the jump circle. We were having Shara jump. She was the tallest - and the toughest, I might add. The ref threw the ball and Shara made a beautiful jump, but instead of tipping the ball, she snagged it out of the air. She exploded out of the mass of girls toward the basket on the wrong end, clutching the basketball like a fullback heading for the goal line.

The ref started blowing his whistle, but the girls paid no attention. Shara kept running with the other nine girls right on her heels. I was sure she was going to shoot at the wrong basket, but I was not concerned she would make it; she hadn't hit a shot in the three weeks of practice. However, I thought it would look stupid for her to do that, so I yelled for her to go to the other end. I needn't have worried. She had no intention of shooting the ball and having someone else get it. She just wanted to keep it for herself - a game of keep-a-way. She turned and headed to the other end of the court, with the rest of the girls close behind. Kathy stopped half way and sat down to rest.

The other girls finally had Shara cornered behind the bleachers, about ten feet outside the out-of-bounds line, circling in on her, like a wolf pack moving in for the kill. The ref was still blowing his whistle and trying to get through the mob, when a girl from the other team jumped Shara. The other seven jumped into the fray, ending up in a giant dog pile. The ball popped out from under them, and one of the girls from the other team grabbed it and was off with the other girls chasing her. Shara was last to get up, but she soon was in hot pursuit as well. Kathy also joined in when they reached mid court where she was resting.

When the girl from the other team found herself cornered, she decided she really didn't want the ball that bad, and threw it over the heads of the other girls. There was a mad scramble for it, and Shara, kicking and shoving, fought the others away and soon had no challengers for its possession. Finally, the ref caught up with Shara, and tried to take the ball from her. She wasn't about to let it go without a fight, and she hung on for dear life until he picked her clear off the ground, at which point she kicked him hard in the shin. The ref was a young, high school boy, and I could see the frustration and pain in his face.

In his anger, and holding his shin and hopping on one foot, he blew the whistle as hard as he could and pointed at Shara. "Foul!" he yelled. At this, Shara kicked him hard in the other shin, dropping him to the floor in pain. That was when I finally decided I should intervene.

"Shara, you can't kick the ref!"

She glared at me. "Did you hear what he called me?! He called me foul!"

"No, he didn't. He said you committed a foul."

"Well, excuse me for not speaking plain English."

I helped the ref to his feet. He glared at me like his pain was my fault. He said the opposing team should have the ball, since Shara traveled and fouled. The buzzer sounded, and the lady running the time clock motioned the ref over. It was the same woman that tricked me into being a coach. She told the ref that they were going to keep the time clock running, even if he blew the whistle, or they would never get through the game.

I looked at the clock, and only one second was gone. I thought that was the most noble thing I had heard yet in what was turning out to be the most chaotic basketball game I have ever witnessed.

A Unique Strategy For A Basketball Game

Coaching the first game for my basket ball team of six and seven year old girls, I found they each had their own family cheering squad, each group yelling at me to make sure their daughter/sister got plenty of playing time. All the girls on the sideline were yelling, "Put me in! Put me in!" Kathy, the only girl on my team that could hit a basket, was already gasping for air after the first minute and yelling, "Take me out! Take me out!"

Half time arrived and the score was still zero to zero. We hadn't even come close to scoring a point, though the other team had. They had a couple of girls that could hit the rim, and I knew it was just a matter of time before one of their shots accidentally went in. It was time to talk strategy. I had tried to explain to my girls about zone and man to man (or girl to girl) defenses, but they didn't understand, so I simply said, "Whatever you do, don't let them get close to the basket."

But I realized that still wouldn't help us make points of our own. I finally hit on a plan. I would station Kathy, unmoving, down by our basket. Shara, who was the fastest, would run the ball to her.

We did our yell and went out for the second half. Kathy positioned herself, and Shara got ready to jump. Shara did a nice tip, but it went into the hands of the other team. The girl from the other team headed toward their basket. She was ahead of everyone and was going for a lay up when Shara tackled her. I then had to explain to Shara that that is not what I meant by keeping them away from the basket.

The ref, who had just about given up blowing his whistle, called a foul. That was ok. We weren't afraid of foul shots. The foul line was outside their shooting range.

Finally, with about thirty seconds left, Trissa jumped on a rebound and came down with the ball. This may not sound like much, but no one ever held onto the ball before. She turned and fired a pass to Jan, and again, a miracle; Jan caught it. Jan threw the ball to Shara and, unbelievably, she caught it, too. She took off full speed for Kathy. The other team stood there awed, I'm sure, by the fact that the ball wasn't bouncing out of bounds.

Shara stopped dead in her tracks by Kathy and handed her the ball. Kathy shot and missed. Shara retrieved the ball and gave it to Kathy. Kathy shot and missed. Shara again retrieved the ball. By this time, the other team had come to life and was headed down the court. I knew if they distracted Kathy at all, she would miss. Just before the others got there, Kathy got off her third shot. The ball rolled around the rim a couple of times and, somehow, fell through.

The crowd on our side went wild. Then the ref had the audacity to claim someone traveled and he invalidated the basket. I don't know what he was thinking; no girl had dribbled through the whole game. I think he was still miffed at Shara for kicking him.

Everyone on our side started booing. The other team was going to get the ball for the last fifteen seconds, so I called a time-out. We may not win, but we weren't going to lose. I told the girls to forget trying to stop them from throwing the ball in from the sideline. I got the five girls with the longest arms, Shara, Jan, Leslie, Emily, and Trissa, and put them into the game. I told them to go to the other end and hold hands in a semicircle around the basket.

They formed the semicircle, facing out as instructed. I was banking on the fact that it would force enough distance that the girls on the other team couldn't hit the basket. It looked like we were forming up for a game of red rover, but it worked. The other team tried to shoot from outside the semicircle and didn't even come close to the rim. The game ended up tied zero to zero. The girls on our team told everyone they won two to zero, but the ref didn't like them and took away their basket.

The other coach came over to visit. "You know," she said, "I've seen some interesting basketball strategies before, but your approach is unique."

Perhaps, but I haven't had any college scouts seek me out. At least not yet.

Facing The Amazons

The season continued, with my team of six and seven year old girls making a lot of progress. Mostly, we learned how to get the ball down the court to Kathy, the only person on our team who seemed able to make a basket. It may have been my imagination, but I think Kathy had lost a few pounds, too, and was almost able to run the length of the court twice. I had been having the girls do pushups, and a few others on the team, besides Kathy, had become strong enough to throw the ball and hit the rim, making it so we had close to a lottery chance of making a basket now and then. We had scored at least one basket per game, making us one of the most feared teams in the league. The only one that was more feared was a team called the Amazons.

Each team had picked mascots. When I asked my girls what they wanted to be called, there were lots of interesting names. There was the "Barbies", but thank heaven someone else already had that. I could just see my resume bragging I had coached the Barbies. I suggested "Munchkins", but they hadn't ever seen *The Wizard of Oz.* My girls finally chose the "Warriors". I'm not sure that works for anyone that is four feet tall, especially girls, but we went with it.

I had grown to love my little team, each and everyone of them. I had seen them change a lot. I still remember the day Leslie showed me that she had cut her Tiger-claw-size fingernails for the game. Her hair was even braided back, though her bangs were still perfectly Miss America curled.

Shara had quit kicking the ref. Mostly. Every once in a while, if he made a call that angered her, she might forget herself, especially if he was within kicking distance.

The girls had all become like daughters to me. I would be in town somewhere and hear a familiar voice yell "Coach!" and turn to see an excited girl running to greet me. As the final game approached, I knew I was going to miss my little team.

As luck would have it, in the round robin tournament, we were to face the Amazons last. We were the only two undefeated teams. I would say that the tension was palpable, but that would definitely be a lie. No one cared, except the usual parent and sibling vocal ensemble.

Word was that the Amazons were really tall, averaging almost four and a half feet, and had even made six points in a game once. As we went to warm up, we saw them on the other end with the usual balls bouncing out of bounds and shooting and missing. But almost every girl on their team was taller than my tallest girl.

They had a lot more natural ability than my girls, but what my girls lacked in height and talent, they made up for in determination. My girls had learned to truly defend. They fought hard, but the Amazons scored the first basket. The Amazons also pressed Kathy hard, but still she was able to make one basket before halftime, putting the score at 2 and 2.

During half time, I talked to the girls. I told them they were all going to have to gain some confidence and try to shoot. That second half, the girls worked hard and played hard against their much taller opponents. At one point, Kathy shot at our basket and missed. Shara fought like a tiger for the rebound. There was no way she could get it to Kathy, as the other team had figured out Kathy was the only one taking shots and had her guarded too well.

"Shoot it!" I yelled. Shara turned and looked at me. Again, I yelled. "Shara, shoot it!"

She turned and just threw the ball at the basket. It wobbled its way to the backboard, rolled around the rim a couple of times, and then fell through, putting us ahead 4 to 2. Our team stood there dumbfounded, as the crowd on our side went wild. I had to call a time out to get my team over the shock. I patted Shara on the back. "Good girl, Shara." She smiled shyly, the first time I think I had seen her smile.

I knew that, whether we won or lost that game, my girls would always be winners in my mind.

It Really Isn't About Basketball, Anyway

My little team of six and seven year old girls played valiantly in their final basketball game of the season, but the superior opponents, each girl six inches taller than my tallest girl, were too much for them. We pulled ahead four to two, but they soon came back and matched our score. With only 20 seconds to go before the final buzzer, the other team scored again.

My team worked hard to get the ball down the court. With just seconds to go, the ball was passed to Kathy. She shot, and the ball rolled around the rim twice, then fell out just as the buzzer sounded.

We had lost, but my girls had never played a better game, and I was proud of them. I brought them close and told them that. I told them I thought they were the greatest girls in the world. We lined up for a final picture. As I looked across my little team, their toothless grins a tooth fairy's dream, I thought they were the most beautiful team ever, and I knew I'd miss them.

As the others scurried off to their families, Shara hung back. She motioned to her mother, her sole supporter at every game. Her mother came over and handed her something. As soon as the other girls were far enough away, Shara shyly approached me. She held out a white envelope.

I knelt down in front of her. "Is this for me?"

She smiled and nodded. It was the first time I found her without words. I opened the envelope and pulled out a beautiful, handmade thank-you card. I could tell by the detail that Shara had spent a lot of time and love on it. My heart felt tight as I read it. "To the greatest coach in the world. Thank you."

Little Shara - my feisty little Shara. I could still remember one game, when she had kicked at one of her own teammates, and I had pulled her out for a while. I recalled the look on her face as she had yelled at me. "You hate me and I hate you, too!"

I had knelt down in front of her and said, "No, Shara, I don't hate you. I actually love you very much, as I do all of the girls, and you are very important to me. I know you are a very good girl and can do better than this, or I wouldn't have taken you out. You have to promise me you will try to do better, and you must apologize to Tanya. If you do, I feel I can trust you, and I will put you back in."

That was the first time I ever saw any soft emotion in this tough little girl. Her big brown eyes filled with tears, and she nodded. I put her back in, and she immediately went to Tanya and apologized. She was much better throughout the rest of the season. She would still strike out once in a while, but she was quick to try to make it right. She started looking toward me often, and I realized she was seeking my approval, so I was always quick to yell, "Good job, Shara!" When I did, her whole countenance would brighten.

Now, as I held the card that she had worked so hard on, my heart tore at me, knowing I might not ever see her again, and knowing she was seeking my love and approval one last time. I looked at her and smiled. "It's beautiful, Shara. Thank you." I thought a minute and added, "You will always remember you are important to me, won't you?"

She didn't say a word, but just nodded and threw her arms around my neck, hugging me tight. I hugged her back, and then she scampered off to join the other girls.

I stood, and Shara's mother approached me. She looked at me with the same big, brown eyes I saw in her daughter - the same smile, the same wisp of hair hanging over her forehead.

"Thank you," she said. "Shara really loves you. She talks about you a lot. Her father abandoned us a couple of years ago, and I've struggled to take care of us. Of course, even when he was here, he was abusive. It's good that Shara can see that there really are good men."

She thanked me once more, and moved to join her daughter. As I looked after her, I felt in my heart that it was I that owed a thanks for the girls whose lives had touched my own, for I had learned more than I had taught, received more than I had given, and been loved even more than I had loved.

For when it was all said and done, it really wasn't about basketball at all.

A Load Of Bull

It started out pretty much like any other project. Old John needed to load his bull into the cattle truck. He'd had the bull for a couple of years, and the bull's offspring were coming of age, so the bull needed to be replaced in order to put new blood into the herd.

Old John backed his truck up to the loading chute and prepared everything. He herded the bull into the pen, and everything was going as planned, until the bull caught sight of the ramp into the truck.

Now, whether that bull had seen too many of his counterparts take a one-way trip in that truck, whether he caught wind of something he didn't like, or whether he had a major aversion to being in a small metal cage on wheels, no one will ever know. But once the bull saw the truck, the whole process ground to a halt.

Old John tried everything. He put grain in the truck to coax the bull in. He got a whip and tried to convince the bull that the truck was a preferred alternative. He tried everything he could think of, but the bull planted his feet and wouldn't budge.

By this time, as often happens in our farming community, everyone driving by had to stop and offer some, not always appreciated, advice. Pretty soon a small crowd of farmers had gathered. Old John, a man of few words, never said anything, though everyone else had an opinion on how to get the job done.

It was suggested that they put a board through both sides of the chute, behind the bull, and then everyone could push. They found the biggest board they could and stuck it behind the bull. Three men got on each side and commenced pushing. But a bull that weighs over a ton can out-push six men who, together, maybe weigh half that.

"Perhaps," suggested James, who had just moved from a big city and bought a nearby hobby farm, "he is just scared. Maybe, if someone would pet him and calm him down, we could get him in the truck."

Everyone stared at him like his rivets were coming loose. Rough and Ready Jackson, chewing on a twig of hay, said, "I'll tell you what, James. You go ahead and climb in there and pet him, and the rest of us will go order your coffin."

Fred pulled up with his sheep dogs. Once he heard the problem, he knew just what to do. He ordered his sheep dog, Butch, into the chute to chase that bull into the truck. Butch looked at Fred like he wondered if Fred had all of his spark plugs firing, but finally went in, barking and growling. Butch came out, flying off the hoof of the irate bull, and when Fred ordered Butch to try again, Butch gave him a sideways look that said, "Why don't you do it yourself, if you think it's so fun."

That was when Rastus showed up. He was a cattleman, if ever there was one. He wore cowboy boots and a cowboy hat, carried a lasso around in the cab of his truck and a saddle in the back, and his whole demeanor bespoke a man in the know when it came to cattle. When he found out the problem, he drawled, "Why, shoot! You just ain't givin' that bull enough motivation 's all. I'll get my motivator out of my truck."

He came walking back with a cattle prod, which most of us call a hot shot - basically a cattle taser. We all stepped aside as he gave that bull a few-hundred-volt shot of motivation. The bull let out a beller, but didn't move. A couple more tries without success, and Rastus was beginning to fear he'd lose face, when he hit on an idea. He reached that motivator in and zapped that bull where no male of any species likes to be zapped.

That bull let out a beller, like a freight train at a busy intersection, and shot forward like a race car coming out of a pit stop, all four hooves squealing in the sand, all horns a-blaring. He pounded up that ramp at a run approaching the speed of sound and continued into the truck without slowing. He hit the truck's front cattle railing, snapping it like a Tinkertoy, and smashed down through the cab of the truck. He came out through the front window, made scrap metal of the hood, and kept going at a dead run through the men and dogs that were scattering for cover. He roared out the yard gate and down the road, heading for the border, bellering and snorting his rage at the injustice he'd received.

As everyone stood around in shock, Old John finally spoke the first words he'd said all day. He turned to Rastus and shook his head. "I think you pushed him just a little too far!"

Dad, The Fix-It Man

My five-year-old daughter came to me and wanted me to put up a "Clo line" for her doll things.

"Don't you mean a clothes line?" I asked.

"No," she responded. "I only want it big enough to hang one clo on."

I had never thought of "clothes" as plural for something before.

I was just about to build it when my four year-old daughter brought me her doll, or at least part of it. The head had come off, leaving only the body. She was in tears about the situation. I told her there was probably a good song we could sing about this predicament. "When you ain't got no-body that wants you. When in life, you just can't seem to get a-head. Then, perhaps, it would all have been better, if you had just spent the whole day in bed..."

It might be debatable whether or not I perjured myself by using the phrase "good song" because, as I continued to sing the bad lyrics, making them up as I went along, she gave me a look that said, "Please tell me I'm adopted and that I don't have any of your genetics."

Well, I calmed her down by saying it wasn't something to lose our heads about. We hunted and found a doll head and put it on the doll body without too much plastic surgery. However, my daughter informed me that it was the wrong head, and I realized that Ken's head does indeed look funny on Barbie's body. The whole thing was enough to drive any-body crazy.

We eventually got ourselves together and got the dolls figured out, or at least their figures together and ourselves figured out. My little daughter gave me a big hug and went off to her world of make believe, with her dolls playing the roles of a brother and sister with high-pitched voices. And thus, my day as "Dad, the fix-it guy", had just started on a Saturday morning.

I don't mind being the fix-it guy most of the time. But recently I have spent about half of my life repairing bike tires. Out where we live, puncture weeds don't just proliferate like mosquitoes, but they actually jump right off the ground and attack without warning. My children come home with their bike tires full of them. I was always fixing flats. Their bikes probably cost me $20 apiece and I would spend about $50 in tubes for each bike each year. I finally got smart and bought some of those solid tubes that don't go flat.

There was, however, one downside. Now that their tires didn't go flat, they rode over everything: nails, porcupines, other siblings, basically whatever got in their path. In particular, they charge out through the worst fields and come back with their tires full of thorns, but totally unfazed.

The problem occurs when they then ride through our garden. I couldn't figure out why the number of weeds in our garden seemed to increase dramatically. What time I saved fixing bike tires went right into weeding the garden.

Though I am no Einstein, I finally figured it out. Now my children are banned from riding their bikes in my garden.

Well, I better be going. My four year-old is back, and one of her dolls has apparently finished paying its taxes, because it's missing an arm and a leg. I need to teach her a song about getting a leg up in the army, and I still have a clo line to build.

When Opposites Attract

My wife, Donna, and I have been married now for 23 wonderful years. When we were engaged, we took a class on courtship and marriage. As part of the course, everyone had to fill out a survey of compatibility. Most of the class had to cajole someone else in to being their partner in the survey, but we conveniently had each other.

Donna and I were the only engaged couple in the class, so the teacher was excited to determine how we compared so he could use our report as an example in his teaching. On the day he brought back the results, everyone could tell he was perplexed about how best to present his material. The students kept badgering him about our report.

"Well," he stalled, "these reports aren't always accurate, you know. They are just a suggestion."

The class pestered him until he finally presented the analysis. On a scale of 0 to 10, 0 being low compatibility and 10 being high compatibility, we had scored around a half a point. I think we might have scored lower, but he didn't dare say so, thinking a small lie was better than the truth.

In reality, we truly are quite different. In our thought processes, we are often on opposite poles of the conceptual planet. We also have great diversities in many other areas as well. Donna is a musician, and I am a mathematician. She grew up in a large city, I grew up so far from anywhere I hardly knew anyone else lived in the same hemisphere. She grew up in California with the sunshine and the ocean. I grew up in Idaho that has two seasons: winter and the Fourth of July. She played clarinet and watched football. I played football and thought I could probably identify a clarinet four times out of five.

The survey didn't deter us, and we married on a spring day in 1984, but we did have to make a lot of adjustments. Donna would say things like, "Would you like the biggest half of the cake?" That would drive me crazy. I would point out to her that it was either "biggest" or "half" but those two sets were exclusionary. I would drive her crazy just mentioning it.

On the other hand, I needed to learn that there are all types of music. I had originally just thought there were two: good music and opera. I learned that music had categories like blues, rock, jazz, classical, etc., and that opera was considered, by some people, to almost be in the good music category, though I have yet to see any scientific proof of that. I by no means desire to insult anyone who likes opera. Everyone has a right to their opinion, no matter how wrong they are.

In one of my classes, I learned that music and math use different parts of the brain. You can decide which part you use the most by considering whether or not you are still wondering what is wrong with someone saying, "the biggest half of the cake", or if you are still pondering what I mean when I say blues and jazz are different.

Anyway, we had people tell us that a right-brained person and a left-brained person were not compatible. I can tell you they are wrong. We have learned a lot from each other. I could talk about it all day long but, right now, I have to go. The biggest half of the cake is calling my name.

Through The Eyes Of Children

✦

It was springtime, and my two youngest daughters had been cooped up in the house all winter and were anxious to get out every chance they could. They were born after we thought we were done having children, and they have complicated our household in many wonderful ways. They have also colored our lives with a tapestry of awareness that we should have had with our other children, but did not always have.

I helped them put their sweaters on, for even though it was May, it was still chilly. Each of them put a hand in mine and we stepped outside for an educational walk through the garden, as I planned to show them the many wonders of spring.

The first sign of spring we came upon were the wild roses that bloom along the ditches and canals near our house. Their fragrance filled the air with a scent that tingled the nose. My two-year-old, Elliana, pointed to them. "What are those?" she asked.

Before I could answer, her four-year-old sister, Heather, responded. "Those," she said, "are called noses. They are called that because they smell so good. But be careful because those sharp things on them are called pokies."

A large orange and black Monarch butterfly landed on the bushes next to us. Heather pointed to it. "Oh, look, Elli, it's a flutterby."

As we stood there watching the 'flutterby', a flock of geese noisily winged its way north in formation above us. Heather pointed to them. "Those are called gooses. The noise they make is honking."

Elliana looked impressed with her big sister's knowledge. "Why are they honking?" she asked.

"Because," Heather answered, with an air of four-year-old wisdom, "they are anxious to get home, and the ones in the front are going too slow, so the ones in the back want them to get out of the road."

As we continued our walk through the garden, a pungent smell filled the air. Heather and Elli both sniffed and wrinkled their noses. Heather turned to her little sister. "That is called a 'stunk', and I'm sure I don't need to tell you why it is called that."

Our walk took us through the strawberry patch that was waking from the cold winter and was starting to put on flowers, like a springtime snow. Heather pointed to them. "Do you know what these are, Elli?" Elli shook her head, so Heather continued. "These are called yum berries. That is their real name, but some people call them slow berries because they take too long before they can be eaten."

As we continued our walk, I just kept quiet and listened to Heather describe the world around us with her vivid imagery and imaginative way. I realized this educational walk was more of an education for me than for them. God gave me eyes to see, ears to hear, a nose to smell, a mouth to taste, and fingers with which to feel. But He gave me children so that I would stop and look, pause and listen, take time out to smell the flowers, be grateful for the flavors of the bounty around me, and reach out and enjoy touching what I see.

Thank you, God, for children.

The Nose Warmer

It's track season - the season when lots of young people are running up and down the street with a look on their face that makes a person think they must be passing a kidney stone. Perhaps it isn't that bad, but I have yet to see any of them smiling.

I remember back to my high school track days. It was springtime, when most young people's thoughts, at least those who are single, turn to something other than track. Our coach had a hard time getting enough runners to field any sort of a team. He promised a varsity letter to anyone who came out for track, competed, and finished the season.

Thus, our ranks were filled with those who only had a vague idea what a track looked like. One such participant was Sam. Sam was the chess club president and part of the chemistry club, but he was determined to earn a varsity letter that he could, one day, brag about to his children.

The day of the first meet arrived, and we were given the standard issue: a pair of nylon running shorts, a nylon tank top shirt, and, of course, a supporter. We had to supply our own running shoes. We went to our assigned lockers to dress. Sam held up the supporter. "Hey, guys, what's this?"

We couldn't believe he hadn't used one in all those years we had P.E., starting clear back in seventh grade. But, apparently, he hadn't, not even for the recent track practices.

Jack was just about to explain to him that it was the underclothes for guys participating in sports, when Lenny, the team comedian, put his hand on Jack's shoulder and interceded. "That," Lenny explained to Sam, "is a nose warmer."

"A nose warmer?" Sam queried further.

"Yes," Lenny continued, not even cracking a smile. Without actually putting it on, but just holding it up in front of his face, Lenny demonstrated how it would fit perfectly over the head and nose, as he continued with his exposé. "It has been clinically shown that an athlete can improve his performance by at least 10% if the air he breathes is warm, much like a car engine does. Thus, by simply trapping your breath and recycling it, you, too, can have a remarkable increase in your stamina and speed."

"Wow! That's cool!" Sam exclaimed.

While the rest of us were coughing and choking the laughter out of our throats, Lenny's face had a serious look, as he continued. "Only the bravest and most determined athletes will wear one, because they are still considered nontraditional. If you want to wear it, I would suggest you only put it on at the last minute, when the gun is fired, so you can take the competition by surprise."

By this time, Sam was dressed and he headed excitedly out to the track, supporter in hand. Most of the team had their heads stuffed in their lockers, trying not to laugh. As soon as Sam was gone, the room exploded. "You don't think he'll really do it, do you?" Jack asked through his guffaws.

"Of course not," Lenny scoffed. "Do you think I would have said it if I thought he would? I'm sure he'll figure it out. If he didn't, it would make the whole team look stupid."

We didn't think any more about it. The track meet progressed as usual. Finally, it came the time for the mile - Sam's event. The runners all lined up. Just as the gun went off, Sam slipped the supporter over his head and was off with the rest. Before the first lap was over, runners were falling like flies, choking and gagging with mirth, as Sam surged past them toward the front. He placed in the top few, higher than he ever would again, due mostly to the fact that most of the viable competitors were about ready to rupture something in their fits of laughter.

When he came trotting off of the track, to be confronted by a red-faced coach, Sam was all smiles. "Wow, Coach! Did you see how well I did? This nose warmer really works!"

An hour or two later, after the track meet was over, all of us, except Sam, were gathered in the dressing room, facing an irate coach.

He glared at us, as he held up the now-famous supporter. "I can take losing! I can even handle us taking last! But, there are certain embarrassments I can't take! And I want to know who the stupid moron is that told Sam this was a nose warmer!"

Uncle Hickory Goes Fishing

Uncle Hickory liked to fish. In fact, he liked to fish so much that he had a hard time waiting until fishing season opened - a real hard time. It was only a week before the big opening day, so he was sure it wouldn't matter if he snuck some fishing in early. Of course, breaking the law is no fun alone, so he convinced Norman to go along. Besides, Norman had a car. Norman was more than a little nervous about the escapade, but the thought of living on the edge made it all the more exciting for Uncle Hickory.

They prepared everything: food to eat, lots of worms, plenty of tackle, and, of course, a bit of beer. Getting off work early, in the pleasant hours of the evening, they made their way up country to a beautiful stream, twenty miles from the nearest point of civilization. At Norman's suggestion, to avoid being easily detected, they decided they would hike over a high ridge and down to the stream on the other side. There, they assumed, it would be much harder for a Fish and Game officer to find them.

The undergrowth was rough, and the pine and jagged rocks took their toll on the lawbreakers, ripping their clothes and skin. It took them over an hour just to reach the ridge of the mountain. They slid down the other side only to find themselves along a thirty foot cliff, overlooking a mountain stream that was swollen from spring melt and was running like a river. Not about to be beaten after their trek through the woods, they decided to fish from the high edge of the cliff.

The water was so turbulent and muddy that the fishing was worthless, but Uncle Hickory didn't care. The fish may not be biting, but the beer was. With each beer, his cast was getting wilder and wilder. Finally, one cast thrown wide hooked into Norman's fishing vest, and when Uncle Hickory threw it forward, he watched as Norman tumbled headlong over the cliff into the raging stream.

Uncle Hickory rushed to Norman's aid. Down the mountainside Norman tumbled with the water, while Uncle Hickory crashed through the brush trying to reach him. Finally, the cliff descended down to the stream, and Uncle Hickory was able to reach out a long branch and pull a sputtering, less-than-grateful Norman to shore.

Norman was soaked and sullen, and the sun was dropping fast in the sky. They had caught no fish, not even a bite; they lost their poles, their food, and their sanity. Defeated, they turned to head back to the car before it was too dark to find their way. They struggled back through the brush, and finally reached the peak of the ridge just as total darkness fell over the countryside.

But what they found waiting for them cast a fear over Norman that made all events up to that point pale in comparison. Down where their car was parked they could see headlights. Norman was sure, in the darkening shadows, that he could make out the ominous sign of the Fish and Game emblazoned on the side of the vehicle.

Uncle Hickory reassured Norman that all would be well. They would just wait until the Fish and Game officer went away, which he surely would do, if they waited long enough. They watched, hour after hour, as the lights continued to glow, until, finally, exhausted from their great exertions, sleep overcame them.

When the morning sun arose, they could see no sign of the feared defender of the law, so they made their way down to the car. There, the full impact of their great adventure was realized as they found their car battery dead from its lights being left on all night.

The Best Mother's Day Gift

When a person gets to be my age, they wonder what they can get their mother for Mothers' Day. My mother pretty well has everything. She obviously has the greatest kids in the world. I mean, look at me - smart, good looking, humble. Okay, so maybe not humble. But I truly can't think of anything she needs. I asked her what she needed once, and she said, "If I needed it, I already got it."

That leaves a person in quite a dilemma as to what gift can be purchased. I suppose I could purchase flowers for her, but everybody does that. I could purchase chocolates, and then, being the thoughtful son that I am, I could hang around when she opened them, in case she needed some help disposing of them. However, these two typical gifts seem so lacking in creativity.

Most people who know me might suggest that is why they are right up my alley. My married daughters get the same big, chocolate candy bar for whatever big occasions comes along - birthdays, Easter, the celebration of their children being potty trained, etc. Of course, they don't complain, mind you, but just once, it might be nice to be known as someone with a little bit of ingenuity.

I was considering one other safe bet. I could get my mother a book. Sure, she has a million books, but there is always another good one that she hasn't read - I'm thinking in particular about the ones I have written. Maybe I could then get her to write a glowing evaluation of it, since no one else I know wants to. But when I asked her if she would like one of my books for Mother's Day, she side-stepped the issue nicely and didn't even bite. "What I would really like is some help around the yard."

So I took my tiller over and tilled her garden, and tilled her garden, and tilled her garden, which is roughly the size of Yellowstone National Park. I dug and moved plants, cut brush, hauled hoses, dug out weeds, reduced poverty and strife, and corrected all the problems in the UN.

When I finished four hours later, my body, that is used to a sedentary life style, was exhausted, but the change in the yard was exhilarating. Everything was clean and neat and looked good, and I felt I had truly given a good Mother's Day gift.

The next day, however, I could hardly convince my muscles to let me get out of bed. I dragged myself to the shower, then to breakfast, then to church. At church, I visited with one of my friends. He was walking like a duck, and every movement seemed to illicit a groan. When I inquired what the problem was, he said he made the mistake of asking his mother what she wanted for Mother's Day.

"Oh, really?"

"Yeah," he continued, with the all-too-familiar story. "She told me she wanted a full day of work on her yards. She had me cut limbs, dig ditches, till the garden, and everything else imaginable. I don't think I've ever hurt so bad in my entire life."

I laughed. "Sounds kind of like my day."

"You think that's bad," he complained. "My wife thinks I ought to do the same thing for her mother next week."

"Good luck," I said encouragingly.

"Yeah, right," he almost growled under his breath. "Next year I'm not going to be stupid enough to ask my mom what she wants for Mothers' Day. Next year I'm just going to buy her a book."

Efficiency in Learning

Every year I give my new students a lecture about learning. I tell them I will try to give them only the homework necessary for them to understand the concepts, and not so much that it just becomes busy work. That way they can still have some sort of social life. In addition, I share a few ideas that may help them to study. This, therefore, is for all students and others interested in learning.

As a student, I paid my own way through college. I always worked one or two part time jobs, and, to save money, I crammed as many as 21 and a half credits into a semester. The half credit was varsity wrestling, which required 4 hours of training per day. A normal load is 12 to 16 credits, therefore, between work and lots of classes, I had to learn to study efficiently.

Math, the subject I teach, is often many students' nemesis. Students tend to procrastinate taking these courses as long as possible, and then tend to put off doing the homework once they are in the class. This results in even more frustration. I tell the students they need to take courses they dislike first, and similar ones as close together as possible. This will help them remember what they have already learned. In addition, there are things they can do to better understand the material and complete their homework more efficiently.

Each of us has probably taken a class where we sit through the lecture and we understand what is being taught. Then time passes and, when we finally sit down to do our homework, we realize that we are clueless about it and can't even figure out our own notes. Some students wonder, at that point, if they ever truly did understand it.

The problem is not actually one of understanding. We learn from psychology that there are two levels of memory: long term and short term. As a former computer science teacher, I often describe this as R.A.M. and hard drive. When a person first learns something, it is in short-term memory (R.A.M.). A person's short-term memory can only hold a certain amount. This means that, as time goes on, it is replaced by other information, and it will be as if they never even attended that class. In order to lock in what they learned into long-term memory (hard drive) a person needs to practice it immediately.

I suggest to my students that if they have a class they struggle in, they need to block out an hour immediately after the class to do the homework. This will help them to process the information to their long-term memory while they still understand it. By doing this, they will learn better, deeper, faster, and more efficiently. I have found, in my own studies, that by following this advice, I could cut my homework time to about a third of what it took before.

I have now done my part to give you a social life. The rest is up to you. Of course, I realize that no matter what I do, some of you won't have a social life, but you can't say I didn't try.

A One-Cow Adoption Agency

I was adopted when I was 16. I really was. However, it's not like you may think. You see, it all started one fall day when a young heifer, Daisy, was having her first calf. She had a hard time in birthing, and we eventually had to partially anesthetize her in order to get the calf born. Unfortunately, the calf did not survive.

My dad said he would take care of the calf, and told me to get Daisy some water, hay, and a bucket of grain. By the time I returned, Daisy was just coming around. Now, animals have some kind of inborn mechanism that tells them they have had offspring, and Daisy was no different. As she looked around and found no other living entity, she, with her cow brain, put two and two together and got something like five, and decided I must be her calf.

As I was coaxing her to eat, she instead, being the good mother she was, decided I should eat first. She struggled to her feet and tried to nuzzle me back to the end that had the milking apparatus. I may not be the fastest gun in the holster, but it didn't take me long to realize what she was thinking.

"No!" I told her. "I'm not hungry, and besides, I hate warm milk!"

She was not about to take no for an answer, so I decided it was time for me to make my exit, and I headed for the fence. She thought otherwise, and, though she was still somewhat wobbly on her feet, she headed to cut me off. She positioned herself between me and the fence and decided I had been a bad calf, determining that she would give me a lickin'. A real lickin', I mean.

She reached out her bristle tongue and scraped it across my face. If you have never experienced a cow licking you before and would like to know what it feels like, just ride a bike at full speed and then jump off face first into gravel. It's about the same sensation.

"You stupid cow!" I yelled, trying to fend off her attack with my arm, as she licked divots into my skin. I was just ready to make a mad break for the fence when she stepped on my foot, pinning it to the ground. The more I tried to push her away, the faster and harder she licked me. These were the days before steel toed shoes, and her 1600 pound weight was grinding my foot into hamburger. The more I pushed her to get her off, the more she leaned on that foot. Finally, exerting all of my strength, I pushed against her, and her hoof rolled off the front of my toes, taking all of the skin with it. I ducked under her head and hobbled at a full gallop to the fence, with her hot on my trail. I dove over the fence, safe from my adopted cow mother.

She put to bellowing, eying me as if to say, "Come back, you stupid calf!" After a day or two, she went hoarse, and I thought she'd have surely forgotten all about me. I decided to take a leisurely stroll through the pasture with my new dog.

There is nothing a cow hates around her offspring more than a dog. Daisy had no sooner spotted us than she was in hot pursuit of my dog. The only problem was, the dog was determined to keep me between him and Daisy. I was sure I was going to get trampled in her over-zealous desire to protect me. We played ring-around-the-cow-pasture for some time, and then the dog made the mistake of breaking away from me. Once separated, Daisy chased him clear back through the gate.

Quick as a flash, she was back. She started nuzzling me toward the rest of the herd. I think she planned to introduce me. As she mooed at the other cows and shook her head at me, as if to say, "meet my new calf", the other cows looked sideways at her like they thought she was a few bales short of a stack.

Her undesired attention continued for a whole year, until she finally had another calf - one that lived. I went out to see her new baby. Suddenly, a look of confusion spread across her face as she looked at me and back at her calf a couple of times. Then she mooed to the other cows, and I could sense she was saying, "Wow, that calf I had last year really was an ugly one, wasn't it?!"

Strawberries, Birds, and Children

There is nothing I enjoy like a good challenge. My wife, Donna, informed me that she didn't think there was any way on this planet that I could grow enough strawberries to ever make her tired of them. Her father grew up on a strawberry farm in California, and his family ate strawberries seven days a week, kind of like we, in Idaho, eat potatoes. He grew to despise strawberries, and once he moved away and had his own family, the word 'strawberry' was considered akin to profanity. Conversely, Donna has an insatiable desire for them.

Therefore, when we finally bought a place of our own, I set out to prove I could grow more than she could ever want. I planted a strawberry patch roughly the size of a small ranch, all laid out in nice, neat rows three feet apart. I planted starts from every kind of strawberry my relatives and friends grew, and added dozens of other varieties found in glossy seed catalogs. I threw in a few more from every local nursery and even pilfered a few unknown kinds that grew wild along the canals. I figured, I alone, with my purchases of strawberry plants that year, subsidized 50% of the U.S. agriculture industry.

I carefully watered, tended, weeded, fertilized, and cared for my precious plants. They put out lots of runners, and, by late summer, the ever-bearing varieties were bright with white blossoms. Soon the little plants were laden with dark green berries which slowly, but surely, grew and started to blush a bright orange, and finally, a mouth-watering red.

I can vividly remember the day I triumphantly carried a handful of strawberries in to Donna. She graciously wanted to share with all of us, but I told her I would have plenty later, when more ripened. She carefully laid out three bowls, her own and one for each of our oldest two daughters. Celese's and Annicka's eyes danced with excitement at the prospect of this new food. Donna equitably counted them out, "One for me, one for Celese, one for Annicka...." She continued this process until each bowl had exactly the same amount. There was one strawberry left over, and she insisted I eat it. We enjoyed our harvest, and my daughters squealed with delight at this flavorful fruit.

I was pleased with my efforts and looked forward to many days of similar enjoyment. However, something happened. Every morning, before heading off to work, I would survey the patch with the intent of picking it that evening. But I would come home to find that all of the ripe berries I had seen earlier were gone. I was sure it was the fault of the birds which sat squawking along the perimeter of the garden, acting as if I was the intruder. I spent a small fortune on every conceivable device to scare them off: owls with glowing eyes and swiveling heads, snakes that seemed to wriggle, and hawks that floated on the breeze. But it never failed that all the berries that were even semi-ripe were picked clean every night when I came home.

I was considering catching one of our cats and staking him out there to earn his keep, when I entered the house and heard a sound that caused me to pause and remember. Celese, in a voice reminiscent of her mother, was saying, "One for me, one for you, one for me, one for you..."

I peeked around the corner and saw my two daughters sitting around a big bowl of strawberries, each of them holding a smaller bowl, as Celese carefully subdivided their day's bounty. It was then that I recalled that they had hardly eaten dinner in weeks. It all came together, and for the first time, I understood that if I was going to win this challenge, I wasn't going to be growing strawberries just for Donna.

Suit Shopping

✦

My daughter, Annicka, brought the young man she was dating to church. That only happens when they are getting serious. My wife, Donna, was also able to arrange for him to sing a musical number, with Annicka accompanying him on the piano. He has a beautiful voice, and sang a song that would fill any heart with emotion. The congregation was deeply moved.

After the service, an older gentleman approached me. He is an old farmer - tough, outspoken, and frank. "Wow! That young man that is with your daughter has a gorgeous voice."

I nodded my agreement as he continued. "You sure don't sing anything like that."

Again I had to agree with him. He concluded. "I would say that, if your daughter marries that young man, she will sure have done a lot better than your wife did."

Well, Annicka did marry that young man. She became engaged to him on the 25th of November, and the wedding was on the 23rd of December. With such short notice, Donna became instantly busy making dresses for our other daughters and our granddaughter. She also realized this wedding provided another opportunity for her, and she was not about to miss it. I was to get a new suit to wear to the receptions.

Now, there is only one thing I hate worse than shopping, and that is trying on clothes. Mix the two, and that is as close to what I imagine the afterlife will be like if I don't make it to heaven. That, alone, motivates me to live an exemplary life.

Anyway, Donna saw that a local store was having a late night sale on suits. I think the reason was so that men like me, who wouldn't normally be caught dead in a clothing store, could sneak in and out under cover of darkness.

Needless to say, I found myself standing in front of a mirror, wishing I was somewhere else. In fact, I was wishing I was anywhere else.

"Wow!" the salesman exclaimed. "That suit makes you look sharp."

"You know how you can tell if a salesman is exaggerating or bulling you?" I whispered to Donna. She shook her head, so I continued. "His lips are moving."

She whacked me playfully.

"Our special today," the salesman added, "is $100 off of one suit, or buy the first suit for full price and get the second for only $25, and we'll even throw in a free tie."

"I hate ties," I replied.

Donna ignored me. "We'll get two suits."

"Wait a minute," I complained. "Why do you think I need two suits? I can only wear one at a time."

"Because I will never get you back in here again," she responded.

She had me there. The salesman didn't want to lose a sale, so he was quick to jump in. "And these suits are the highest quality. Why, a suit like this will last you 20 years."

I multiplied 20 by two, and figured I would never have to buy another suit in my life, so I agreed. I endured the changing and prodding for tailoring, and finally thought I was done.

The salesman grinned. "Now, about some shoes."

"What?!" I growled. "There is nothing wrong with my boots."

The salesman looked at Donna and pointedly ignored me. "Cowboy boots really don't go well with a suit of this quality."

Donna nodded her agreement. I wasn't going to give in without a fight. "I can't try on shoes, I have holes in my socks."

She turned back to the salesman. "We need a new pair of socks, too."

Thus, I found myself trying on stiff, shiny shoes, while my friendly, comfortable boots were shoved into a sack, like long forgotten friends.

I was finally done. "Well, how do you feel?" Donna asked.

"Do you really want to know?"

"No," she answered. "It was just a rhetorical question."

When I got home, there was a message to call Annicka. When I finally got through to her, she said, "Dad, there's been a change of plans. We want you to wear a tux at the reception. You will need to come down early so you can go to the rental store and try it on."

All I can say is that it's a good thing I love her.

There Is A Deep Understanding After The Fact

This summer, as we prepare to perform one of my plays, **April Fools**, my mind wanders back a few years to its first production. Our group, the *Drama Source Players*, works in a community theatre setting and always brings together a variety of people, all of whom are willing and eager to give up their own free time for the thrill of the stage. For me, the enjoyment is more about the friends I make than the excitement I feel.

That summer was no different. We had a mixture of those who had been with us before, as well as new people who joined our group and became lifelong friends. I can never see this play performed without thinking of one wonderful young lady named "Tana". She had just graduated from college in theater and was home for the summer. She was dazzling in her tryout, and established herself for lead roles in two of the plays we produced that summer. She had a lot more training than any of us, and quite a bit more talent than most of us.

We all had a fun summer together, performing one drama and one melodrama. Soon the long nights of practice gave way to the, seemingly, short nights of performance. We had our traditional opening night watermelon bust, as well as our Saturday matinee pizza party. We had fun awards for those with the most humorous mess-up, lots of laughs for the biggest costume gaffes, and pleasant times just getting to know each other as we sat around and ate caramel popcorn after each night's performance. Tana joined us and fit right in, though at times she seemed somewhat distant, and I wondered if she were wishing for the more professional groups she had performed with and directed in the past.

The summer was over far too quickly, and we said our good-byes to our friends as we promised to keep in touch, and asked those available to make plans for another production the next summer.

One year quickly rolled into the next, and we were once more casting for our summer productions. We hoped that Tana could join us, and attempted many times to contact her, but to no avail. She was never home, and no one ever returned our calls. After some time we decided she must have made the determination to only work in more professional groups.

We started our rehearsals and moved forward. One night, during the week of dress rehearsal for our first production of the summer, we received some horrible news: Tana had taken her own life. Our emotions ran too high to attempt further practice that night, so we set out to purchase flowers for her family.

As I sat at her funeral a few days later, listening to her life history being read, much of it written by herself, I learned things I had not understood before. She had suffered from severe depression all of her life. Though we had wondered if she was disappointed that we were not as professional as she was used to, I learned that she had loved the friendship and acceptance she had found in our group to the extent that she wondered, in turn, if she was good enough for us. During the reading, her own words expressed that her summer performances with us provided the most enjoyable time of her entire life. When that was said, my heart choked within me.

I wondered whether she might still be with us if we had just tried a little longer and harder to get her to join us that summer. I considered a lot of "what if's", but, of course, to no avail. It is much easier in hindsight to understand what someone is thinking, but by then it is too late to do anything about it.

There is one thing I do know ahead of time. As I step on the stage this summer, to perform this play which Tana loved so much, I will be saying within my heart, with all the love we felt for her, "This one, Tana, is for you."

The Real Purpose Of A Hometown Parade

Two things happened that year that changed everything: my cousins came up from California, and it rained on July 3rd. When it was hay hauling season, nothing interfered, and we had never taken the Fourth of July off before. But a person can't haul hay until it is thoroughly dry. Thus, for the first time, my dad declared it an unofficial holiday.

We decided to take our cousins to the community celebration in Ashton. I have always liked small towns, and Ashton is one of my favorites. It has a main street about six blocks long, unless you don't count the grain elevators, which would deduct two blocks. There are a couple of small, handmade furniture stores, a theater, some craft stores, one café, and a bar. That is pretty much the main street.

Shopping in Ashton back then consisted of one all-purpose gas station-grocery-hardware store. We are not talking WalMart; we are talking it only carried one variety of anything, and if a person didn't like it, well, that was just too bad.

In Ashton, everybody knows everybody, and those they don't know they are related to. There is no stop lights or crosswalks; Ashton doesn't need them. Why, there isn't that much traffic, and people cross the road anywhere they darn well pleased, even if there is traffic coming, which there almost never is.

The parade that day started right at ten, with a police car leading the way. This was not because it looked official, but because people stood in the middle of the street and visited, and the police car was to get them to move to the sidewalks. Sometimes they still didn't move, and the police officer would give his siren a blast. Then the people would yell, "All right,

Thompson, don't get shovey! Don't get shovey!"

My cousins were from California, and in their depravity, had never seen a real home-town parade. Blair, who was closest to my age, let me know that this definitely was no Rose Parade. I didn't know what a Rose Parade was, but it sounded boring, and I didn't like him bad-mouthing my home town.

As the parade went on, people would stroll back and forth from one side of the street to the other between the floats. Blair had the nerve to suggest that it wasn't proper, but my dad said, "A parade is only as good as the number of friends you can meet."

There were the veterans carrying the flag, a band that played an almost-recognizable tune, the pretty drill team girls, which my older brothers especially liked, and then the floats. One of the drivers had forgotten to drop his food off at the baked food sale. He just parked in the middle of the street, hopped out, and took his food to the table. Someone yelled, "I hope you weren't the one that baked that, Joe!" and another called out, "Hey, Joe, what's the problem? Won't your Chevy go? Maybe you should get a Ford!"

There were politicians in big cars with signs on the side that my brother told me all said, "Vote for Dufus", no matter who was in the car.

I especially enjoyed the horses and the farm equipment. Blair had the audacity to announce that it was unconventional to have farm equipment in a parade. I just rolled my eyes and wondered what planet he was from. There were quite a few other entries, but the parade only lasted about 20 minutes. "Is that it?" Blair gasped.

"No," someone answered, "just wait." Soon it came back from the other direction.

Blair laughed, "Great! We get to see it twice just to make it long enough to be counted as a parade. And there are no stars or anything."

I was ticked off. "You want stars, I'll show you stars!" I growled, grabbing him by the nape of the neck, but my dad intervened. About then, the parade ended, and my dad took us to buy a hamburger and a root beer float.

It wasn't long before I grew up and was gone for several years to New York, working on a graduate degree, and marrying a beautiful lady from Los Angeles. The summer I returned, I took my family to the Ashton parade. As I ran into friends there, for the first time in a long time, I felt I was truly home. My dad was older and walked slowly with his cane, and it was now me who was buying hamburgers and root beer floats for my parents and my own children. I talked to lots of people I hadn't seen in years.

The funny thing is, I can't remember much about that parade, but I guess it doesn't matter. After all, "A parade is only as good as the number of friends you can meet."

When Relationships Go Sour

⁜

Jo wasn't speaking to me, and though I relished the tranquility, I found myself in our director's office explaining the situation.

I had been the top person in our area until she came. But she was better than me at almost everything from the moment she arrived. That didn't bother me as much as how she flaunted her supposed superiority. I was 20 and she was 22, and the fact that we had to work together at times just made it worse. If I did 15 presentations in a week, she did 15 and a half. If I did 17, she did 17 and a half. I never figured out how a person did a half of a presentation to Mr. John Doe Public, but she always reported a half of a presentation more than me. It didn't help that she carefully waited to find out how many I reported before she reported hers.

Another young man in our group suggested I should, sometime in the future, consider marrying her, since, he said, I was the only one he knew that could stand up to her. I told him that when I was young, my mother had washed my mouth out with soap for saying things that weren't nearly that vile. To be honest, my relationship with Jo truly did have everything that a good love-hate relationship would have - everything except the love.

To make matters worse, those to whom we reported had the audacity to suggest that perhaps our enmity toward one another could be diminished by finding some outside activity that we could enjoy together - in a group setting so we didn't kill each other. I thought that was the most dim-witted idea that I had ever heard. Why would I want to spend my free time with her? But Jo thought it was brilliant. I'm sure she latched onto it as another chance to annoy me - and again show her superiority.

Thus, the test of my patience was brought to a head when, on an off-work day, I organized a basketball game for some of the young men in our group. I'm not sure how Jo found out about our game at the local YMCA. If I ever do find out, somebody is in big trouble. But the fact is, she showed up with another reluctant young woman in tow.

I asked her what she was doing, and she informed me that she was there to play basketball with us. I told her we had planned to play with just the eight of us that were already there. She said it was a free world, and I wasn't king, and she could play if she wanted. I told her the teams were already even, but she said that was why she had brought someone else ready to play. I was at a loss, and looked at the other young men. They just shrugged. I finally agreed, partially because athletics was the one place I shined. When she told the other young woman to be on my team, and she, glaring at me, joined the opposing team, I warmed to the thought of teaching her a little lesson in humility.

She stood about five foot tall to my five foot ten inches, though she was indeed a ball of fire and a good player. But I had played a lot of street ball in New York, and our team was gradually, but steadily, pulling into a huge lead, which did not play well on Jo's temperament. The longer the game went, the darker her mood became. At one point, when she attempted a shot and I knocked it forcefully to the floor, I thought I was going to see her lose her barely-controlled temper, but she restrained herself with little more than a glare and a growl.

But then came the moment when she thought she had a free break the full length of the court. As she dribbled the ball at full speed, I outraced her and, just before she reached the basket, I made a clean steal and headed to the other end for an easy lay-up. I turned to gloat, only to find her bearing down on me like a miniature locomotive. She slammed into me, but, still robust from my years in athletics, I watcher her only bounce off, landing on her back on the floor. She jumped to her feet, fists clenched, yelling, "That is no way to treat a lady!"

Forcing a fake, calm smile I replied, "When I meet one, I'll remember that."

"And that, Sir, is when she took a swing at me. And she hasn't spoken to me since."

Sleep Apnea

My wife, Donna, told me I really wasn't sleeping well. Sometimes people like to point out the obvious. However, we had just read an article that told us married men live much longer than single men, and most of it seemed to indicate that the reason was because their wives looked out for their health.

I knew I wasn't sleeping well, but what was a person to do about it? Donna said I stopped breathing a lot, and needed to see a doctor.

Therefore I found myself in the office of an Ear, Nose, Throat, and Mustang Car specialist. He was a good, thorough doctor, and he found much of my airway was blocked by my tonsils. Tonsils are those things that a person normally has removed when they are an innocent child. But I didn't, and now they had grown to roughly the size of basketballs. Nonetheless, before they could be extracted, the insurance company wanted a "sleep study".

I soon found myself in a room in which I was supposed to spend the night. A woman hooked more wires to me than can be found under the hood of a car, looking for a similar diagnosis that a mechanic would, I'm sure. I had wires on my chest, head, legs, arms, and everywhere else that a bare spot could be found or shaved.

After a quick review of what they were looking for, she left me alone saying, "Have a good sleep."

"Was that supposed to be a joke?" I called after her as she shut the door. And, indeed, I found that a sleep study is totally misnamed, at least the sleep part. Every movement during the night made me feel like I was wrapped in a ball of twine. Finally, the night ended with me wide awake at about five a.m. When the sleep enforcer finally entered my room, she said,

"You seemed kind of restless all night."

"Me?" I growled. "How could that be? I'm used to being tied to my bed when I sleep."

Well, the study finally came back, and the surprising result was: "YOU DON'T SLEEP TOO WELL!"

I thought that was an amazing analysis for nearly $1000.

It is the job of the insurance company to spend a person's money on frivolous things; therefore, they wanted to see if more air would help me. Apparently, it is not obvious to them that a lack of air is detrimental to the continued state most people prefer - mainly, living.

Though the doctor reported that my tonsils "inhibited" my airway, the insurance company insisted I get a breathing machine. Every night I had to be tethered to it. Basically, every time I breathed in, it inflated me like a balloon. It was better when we got the control corrected from 150 psi to around 5, a normal breathing setting, but I still sounded like Darth Vader on steroids, locked in a closet. They said they wanted to find out if the oxygen level in my blood was better when I slept. I don't know how they were supposed to determine that, since I could never sleep. By the end of the month, I was tired, grouchy, and ready to turn to the dark side.

At the end of the study, after hundreds more dollars were spent, they came to another important conclusion: "YOU NEED TO HAVE YOUR TONSILS OUT!"

I thought I had finally come to the end of this great adventure, but, alas, I had only come to the beginning.

Preparing For Tonsil Surgery

Before I went in for tonsil surgery, the doctor said I should put things in order. It sounded so final, like I was going to die, or something. He just said I wouldn't want to do anything for a couple of weeks afterward. I laughed. "I've never had a surgery that could keep me down for very long. I'm sure I'll be up and around shortly." He just rolled his eyes.

My surgery was just a few days before Mothers' Day and I didn't even bother getting my wife a gift ahead of time. Why should I? I was sure that within 24 hours I'd be right back to my normal activity. Sure, I would hurt a little, but I could endure that.

The day was on me sooner than I expected. It has always been interesting to me that a hospital has a person arrive for surgery at 4:30 in the morning, during that part of the day when a normal person is still in bed. They also told me not to eat anything for at least twelve hours or so. I'm sure the purpose for all of this was so I wouldn't be thinking straight and couldn't really consider what I was getting myself in to. I've always been amazed that they tell me to have no food, and they make it so I have no sleep, and then they wonder why I am irritable.

After I was settled into a room, they had me dress in a backless gown so I would be too humiliated to try to flee, then they asked me lots of questions like, "Is anyone in your family allergic to anything? Has anyone in your family ever met anyone that is allergic to anything? Have you ever sued a hospital before? Do you have insurance? Has your insurance ever paid any hospital bill without complaining?" Don't answer yes to that last question or they think you're lying and they start over.

Next come the nurses. One came in to check all my vital signs like my heart, lungs, and impulse to flee. Another nurse joined her, and had enough needles to start her own MASH unit. At this point, the nurse checking my blood pressure said, "Did you know your blood pressure is really high?" "Yes," I answered, "but it wasn't until I saw all of those needles."

Once the first nurse had verified I was truly still alive, the second nurse started poking the needles into me to see if she could remedy that situation. Nonetheless, when she finished, I had not yet crossed over to the other side, though I felt my day of judgement must be getting near. Having survived the first attack, the surgery still loomed on my horizon. After turning on the IV to about 20 gallons per second, the nurse told me to just relax, and she left.

Soon I was facing another dilemma. When nature calls, I really hate making it into a public event, but I was attached to so many machines that I knew I, and all of the little R2-D2's that were with me, wouldn't fit into the bathroom. I therefore had no choice but to push a button and announce my intentions to the world.

Shortly, a nurse arrived, and helped me disconnect some of the little mechanical parasites, while I had to drag the others with me. Finally, more relaxed, I settled in for the long wait, until I was queued up for departure to anestheticville.

This wait was their last phase of prepping me for surgery. They left me for about five hours in a room with a TV that had a broken remote and was locked into endless "Barney" reruns, so that if I did happen to die, I would be grateful. Once my IQ has dropped 50%, due to giggling dinosaurs, I was finally ready for surgery; reckoning nothing worse could happen to me.

Going In For Tonsil Surgery

Since I finally had the official result from my insurance company, I was ready for my tonsils to come out. The doctor said they wanted to give me the whole load. I was going to get my tonsils out, my nose realigned, my tongue cauterized, and my cat neutered. Sorry about that last one - wrong list.

Anyway, the doctor suggested for someone of my age it might be best to do it in three surgeries. I always hate that phrase "for someone of your age". It makes me feel like I have one foot in the grave. I was a rough, tough athlete when I was younger, so I told him I wasn't afraid of a little pain.

"Do you want to go without anesthetic, too?" he asked sarcastically. I just laughed, but he didn't seem to be smiling.

But how bad could it be? Just a few months earlier, I had been in the hospital with my two little girls when they got their tonsils out. Elliana was three and Heather was five, and they didn't seem to have any problems. Oh, sure they were a bit sore for a day, but they soon warmed to the idea of eating all the ice-cream they wanted.

They had been funny when the nurse had given them some medicine to drink to help their anesthetic work better. Each had responded in a different way. Elli relaxed and was like a limp Raggedy Ann doll. Heather kept hallucinating. She kept wanting to sit up in her bed and "catch the pretty stars" that she said were floating around her head. She would sit up and reach out into the air, only to flop back onto her pillow.

I had a lump in my throat as they wheeled them out. They seemed so small on those big, white beds. But soon they were back. Elli wanted out of her bed to curl up in my arms. She whimpered for a couple of hours, but when her mother brought me French Fries for lunch, she was upset that she couldn't have any and soon was her old self.

Heather hardly seemed fazed by the surgery at all. She found the remote for the TV by her bed and kept rolling through the channels, only pausing long enough to watch **Mr. Roger's Neighborhood**. We only pick up two channels at home and, at the hospital, she had about 50.

Having watched their quick recovery, I couldn't imagine I had anything to dread, even "at my age". Therefore, three months after them, I found myself lying on a white bed with people all around me, wearing masks to conceal their identity and protect them from later retribution. One man came over and introduced himself in mumblease from behind his mask as the anesthesiologist. He told me they would be putting me to sleep soon. As the medicine was administered and I started to get sleepy he told me he had a friend who had been through the same thing two weeks earlier.

"Did he think it was all worth it?" I asked.

He shrugged. "I don't know. He still won't speak to me."

By then it was too late for me to back out and, with that thought, the black drifted over me and I was wheeled off to the hospital torture chamber.

Getting Tonsils Out

The beauty of modern medicine is its ability to make a person go to sleep, then wake up in more pain than he could ever have imagined he was capable of enduring. As I started to wake up from getting my tonsils out, there was a nurse sitting next to me talking on a cell phone.

"I tell you, Gladys, if you add a dash of salt and lemon pepper and cook at 350 degrees, they can be downright tasty."

I still had tonsils on my mind, and the thought of cooked tonsils almost made me gag. I'm sure she was talking about something sensible like Rocky Mountain Oysters or pig intestines, and not tonsils, but my regurgitation response was feeling stronger than a bird feeding its young.

As I started to move, everyone wanted to talk to me, but my throat felt like it was stuffed tight, and I know my nose truly was. An orderly leaned over me and smiled.

"How are you feeling?"

"Mrugrmeljke," I answered.

"Good!" he said.

What I had said wasn't anything close to "good", but what I had felt like saying can't be written in a family newspaper. They had me strapped to my bed, afraid I would run away if I got the chance. They wheeled me down to a room where my wife, Donna, was waiting for me.

She smiled. "How are you feeling?"

"Mrugrmeljke," I answered.

"I didn't catch that," she said.

I thought that was probably a good thing.

The doctor came in and leaned over me. "How are you feeling?"

"Mrugrmeljke."

"Good. Enjoy it while you can," he said. "When the localized pain medicine wears off, which it will, almost as if in an instant, you might hurt a little."

He left, and about fifteen minutes later the localized medicine did wear off just as he said. He got that part right. With regard to the part about hurting a "little", he and I weren't even in the same dictionary.

They gave me a little button and told me to squeeze it if I hurt. If it had been a cow I would have milked ten gallons out of it in under five minutes, but I still didn't feel any better. They forgot to tell me it only gave me a limited amount.

Later, the doctor came back to check on me again. "Still feeling like that tough athlete?" he smirked.

I thought that was a dumb question. Of course I wasn't - he was still alive, wasn't he? If I had been feeling tough, with the way I hurt, his survival status might be questionable - an obvious case of self-defense on my part.

"You know," he continued, "One of your tonsils was totally infected and smelly. It should have been removed long before this. Didn't any of your friends ever tell you you had bad breath?"

I didn't know why he was asking me these questions since I couldn't talk, but obviously a person had to have friends first, in order to have them tell you such things.

The nurse brought me popsicles just as Donna and my two youngest daughters came back to visit me. I didn't want the popsicles, so Heather and Elli dutifully helped me dispose of them. "See, Daddy," Heather, said between licks, "it isn't so bad."

I couldn't eat anything all day, so the nurse kept the IV fluids pumping at about 20 gallons per minute. I think my two little girls probably emptied the equivalent of a Baskin-Robbins store in my behalf.

"Look at the bright side," Donna said. "You should lose weight." Even that didn't work. When I finally got home, I had more fluid in me than a city water tank, and the scale said my weight was up ten pounds. At that point I was still wondering if a bright side would ever appear.

Recovering From Tonsil Surgery

I couldn't sing all that well before my tonsil surgery, and I had hoped the surgery might help that. But when I came out of the surgery, I was more concerned with the thought that I was going to die. Then, after the powerful localized pain killer wore off, I was afraid I was going to live. The only time I had ever hurt that bad was when a horse kicked me where no male of any species likes to be kicked. That time the whole world had begun to spin, and I thought I was going to pass out. When I finally got my bearings and my surroundings started to stabilize, I was a new man, more or less - probably less.

Anyway, after about twelve hours of being awake following my tonsil surgery, once the doctor was confident all bleeding had stopped, I was paroled to go home. I wobbled my way into a wheelchair, and the nurse deposited me on the curb to pull myself into our waiting van.

I must admit that it was nice to leave the smell of disinfectant behind. I could hardly wait to get home and lie down. My wife, Donna, kept trying to encourage me. "At least you don't have to use that CPAP machine anymore."

The CPAP machine was the machine I had used at night to increase my oxygen level while I slept. I think the letters C-P-A-P are some kind of abbreviation. I'm quite positive it is a terrorist organization, something akin to Al-Qaeda. I would wake up every morning with its air hose wrapped around me, like a giant python trying to choke me.

The five days prior to Mothers' Day came and went, and I still hadn't felt good enough even to get my wife a present. I tried the strong pain killer the doctor prescribed and found a small side-effect: I quit breathing. I would relax so much that I would go to sleep, but when I did, I also relaxed enough to stop the process of inhaling. For those who don't know, this can be detrimental to a person's health. Donna realized I was doing this, and for six hours, until the medicine wore off, she would shake me when I began to drowse and I had quit breathing.

But it had made me feel so good I kind of wanted to take some more. I tried to convince her that not breathing was only a small, incidental result compared to the pain, but she hid the medicine, and I found myself relegated to using ibuprofen, since I had also had strange reactions to other painkillers.

After about two weeks, I finally started to feel like I was going to live again. There were some interesting results, however. The first one was, after I didn't sleep for two days straight getting rid of the water the nurses had pumped into me with the IV, I lost thirty pounds. I considered patenting it as a major weight loss method. I would create a product that makes a person's throat so sore he couldn't eat if he wanted to. Either I'd be rich or sued into oblivion.

The second effect of getting my tonsils out was that my voice quit cracking. I was one of those guys in high school that always had a voice that would squeak at the most inopportune times: asking a girl out, cheering for a teammate, or singing a solo in front of the whole student body. It caused great glee for my friends, especially as I was winning the state championship in wrestling, and my voice was jumping to an octave obtainable only by members of the Vienna Boys' choir. The big problem was, even though I learned to control it somewhat, it continued to occur my whole life, until that day I got my tonsils out. Once they were out, there wasn't any sudden break in my voice, just gradual change from morning until night. I would start out the day with my voice in the gravelly low registers that sounded like a Kenworth Truck grinding its gears down a steep grade, or a bull frog with a hornet stuck in his throat. My voice didn't loosen up until about noon.

Then came the first chance to test out my singing. At an early morning choir practice, the church choir director stopped the music and looked at me. "Daris, can't you take that bass part up about two octaves?"

"Sure," I responded, "if you give me about six more hours."

"Then," grinned one of my fellow choir members, "perhaps you would consider just mouthing the words."

I guess my singing hasn't changed much.

The Giant Canvas Of A Child's Heart

I worked for two years to build on our new addition. It was a 22 foot by 24 foot sunken living room with a foyer and a half bath. I had hoped to have it contracted out so I wouldn't have to build it, but, when we asked for bids and the contractors found out how much we could spend, I think they put call blocking on our phone number so we couldn't bother them.

After two years of hard work, smashed fingers, lots of cuts and scrapes, and more than one nasty fall, the room was finally ready for the carpet. This was my wife's choice. When it comes to paint and carpet, I don't even like to go there. I'm still trying to understand why pink and red don't go together. After all, they are in the same realm of the color spectrum. But half of the time, when I get my littlest daughters dressed for church, my wife has to redress them for proper color coordination.

For our new living room, my wife had this wonderful dream of a room where everything was always perfect when company drops by. For that reason, she chose a nice, off-white carpet. I think when she did, either she met a real good salesman, or she totally forgot that we have children. Either way, when she settled on that color and I asked her about it, she just said, "It will be all right. We won't allow the children to take food into that room."

I started to tell her I had also heard a good joke, but I held my tongue, and a few days later the carpet installer came. I have to admit that the carpet was beautiful. It made the room look elegant. The only thing that would have helped is if we could have afforded furniture.

Our children were happy in this new room with its great expanse. They would roll and play on the carpet endlessly.

Then one day, when I came home from work, I was met outside by my three-year-old, Elliana, and my four-year-old, Heather. One had a blue marker and one had a red.

"Daddy! Daddy!" Heather said excitedly. "Come see the picture we made."

They slipped their hands into mine and we walked into the house. As I stepped into the foyer, Heather pointed at the new room and said, "Didn't we do a good job?"

I looked at the new white carpet, and there was the biggest blue and red smiley face I had ever seen, or, at least, what was supposed to be a smiley face. It stretched most of the way across the room on all sides, about 10 feet in diameter. It must have taken them hours and half a dozen markers.

I know at this point that I should have looked down at my two smiling angels and said, "What a nice smiley face you have drawn. My, you definitely have a career in art ahead of you - perhaps decorating train cars." But instead, what came out was more like a strangled scream. My wife quickly appeared to see what caused my consternation, and she gasped at what she saw. She looked like she was about to cry, seeing what had happened to her dream room.

After conspicuously confiscating the markers and making sure all others were out of reach, I obtained some carpet cleaner and some old towels and started to scrub. I grumbled audibly and worked for four or five hours that evening, even skipping dinner. My wife suggested that we might want to rent a steam cleaner. "Why would I need to do that?" I grumbled. "I'm already a steamed cleaner."

When it was bed time, my two little daughters approached me

cautiously, a book in hand. It was our routine every night to have me read them a story, coach them on brushing their teeth, help them with their prayers, and tuck them into bed. But this time, as I was still finishing up the last of the carpet cleaning, I was still mad, and gruffly told them they would have to forgo a story.

They knew how upset I was, and didn't argue. By the time their teeth were brushed, I had done everything I could, and the carpet only showed the faintest outline of a smiley face. As Heather said her prayers, she prayed, "... and help Daddy not be mad and still love us..." Suddenly, I felt like a real heel, and the problem with the colored carpet paled in significance with what really mattered.

"Sweetheart," I said to her after she finished her prayers, "your daddy will always love you."

"No matter what?" she asked, as tears glistened her eyes.

"No matter what," I answered. As my two little girls sniffled softly, I pulled them onto my lap. I figured they needed a hug. I know I did.

Glue Cakes And Black Bears

✦

Aunt Hazel was never known for her cooking. It is true that certain things turned out quite well. She could make a mean gooseberry pie, but the mean part was that it came back to haunt you an hour or so after you ate it.

But there was one thing she was infamous for, and that was her cakes. She had never made a cake that was edible, although she was determined, and kept trying.

One of her unsuccessful attempts occurred when hers and Uncle Hickory's family was young. They decided to take a family trip into the woods. This was back in the days when, as a person traveled through Yellowstone Park, the black bears would come right up to the car. The bears also undauntedly came right into the campgrounds. I'm sure, however, it was the episode with Aunt Hazel that turned the whole bear population into the untrusting creatures they have since become.

You see, as soon as the family set up camp, Aunt Hazel decided to bake a cake. It was Uncle Hickory's birthday after all. If Aunt Hazel wasn't a stellar cook with a stove, her cooking in the out-of-doors came close to violating every known environmental law on the books.

Uncle Hickory laid out a roaring fire while Aunt Hazel prepared her "secret recipe". The reason it was a secret was because she tried to do it out of her head from remembering how her mother cooked. It should be known that Aunt Hazel's mother was indeed a good cook. It was just that Aunt Hazel had never felt it was important, and therefore had just learned it haphazardly, thinking she could pull it from memory when needed.

Once the fire had burned down to nice coals, Aunt Hazel put her mixture into it. The smell that emanated from the pan was about that of hot tar and turpentine and it looked like it smelled. It bubbled and brewed like a witch's cauldron, then hardened into a gooey, charcoal-looking concoction.

After a dinner of burnt hot dogs, Aunt Hazel brought out the "cake". Everyone looked at it, reluctant to be the first victim to taste its contents. Aunt Hazel figured Uncle Hickory should get the first taste, since it was his cake. He felt that, since it was supposed to be his celebration, he should be spared from this cruelty. Nonetheless, he got a knife and dutifully tried to cut out a slice. That was as far as it went. Once the knife was inserted, the caked wrapped itself around it and refused to let go. Uncle Hickory got a fork to try to free the knife, but the fork also became stuck. After struggling in vain for a half hour to free the utensils, Uncle Hickory disposed of the cake into a trash receptacle. The family sang happy birthday and sat down to raspberry jam spread on hot dog buns for Uncle Hickory's festivities.

They had just settled into bed, and were barely drifting off to sleep, when a ruckus in the campground brought them to immediate alert. Garbage cans were banging and a bear was bawling, until the whole camp was in turmoil. Uncle Hickory looked out to see a yearling black bear with his teeth sunk deep in the cake. He was bawling and rolling among the garbage cans, knocking over everything. The bear tried to pull the cake from his teeth, only to get his claws stuck in it. The more he tried to get free, the more stuck he became.

The bawling brought other bears. One, apparently the young bear's mother, obviously thinking the cake was attacking her baby, tried to slap the cake away from him. But the cake was stuck tight, and each powerful swipe only sent the young bear tumbling into more garbage cans. Finally, with great ferociousness and anger, the mother bear started shredding the cake to bits, stopping only to growl in anger when it would stick to her.

Uncle Hickory's comment that he knew how the mother bear felt brought glares from Aunt Hazel. When the cake was dismantled, the bears disappeared into the night, never again to trust humans.

And that was how Aunt Hazel, single-handedly, cured bears of wandering into camp grounds to dine on food prepared by humans.

If you enjoyed our book, we'd appreciate a review on Amazon.

http://amzn.com/1449543510

Would you like to see Life's Outtakes column running in your local paper or magazine? Suggest it to the editor. If an editor runs the Life's Outtakes column due to your suggestion, we will send you one of Daris Howard's books, of your choice, signed by the author. Find out more at:

http://www.darishoward.com

Read other stories, purchase more books, or sign up for a short story each week by going to

http://www.darishoward.com

Other books
by
Daris Howard

Daris Howard Amazon page: http://amzn.com/e/B004H76UGK

Life's Outtakes books
(52 humorous and inspirational Stories in each book)

1. When The World Goes Crazy - Life's Outtakes Year 1

2. All's Well Here - Life's Outtakes Year 2

3. When Life Is More Than We Dreamed - Life's Outtakes Year 3

4. Nothing But A Miracle - Life's Outtakes Year 4

5. Singing To The End Of Life - Life's Outtakes Year 5

6. It's Ninety Percent Mental - Life's Outtakes Year 6

Other Books

The Three Gifts - http://amzn.com/1449961436
A beautiful Christmas story about three young men who are convicted of mugging little children for their Halloween candy. Instead of sentencing them to jail, as is expected, the judge sentences them to 100 hours of community service babysitting at the Women's Crisis Center.

They were prepared for jail, but they were not prepared for what was in store for them as the children opened their eyes and hearts and changed their lives.

Super Cowboy Rides - http://amzn.com/1937178021
Meet six-year-old Tommy Johnson, Super Cowboy and Super Story-teller. When Tommy explains why a boy needs a dog for a pet instead of a cat, he wins everyone over with his down-to-earth and humorous view of the world. But once Tommy starts school, things get complicated. He gets put in the lowest reading group and told to stay in the back of the classroom. He is picked on by teachers and mocked by classmates. When tragedy strikes, Tommy must carry a burden beyond what any first-grader should have to face. In the process of dealing with his grief, Tommy learns the meaning of true friendship.

Essence Of The Heart, The Royal Tutor -
http://amzn.com/1479392189

Mystery, Intrigue, And Clean Romance!

When he is called before the queen, Jacob, the handsome, young Captain of the Royal Guard, is sure it is to discuss the baffling increase in assassination attempts against the royal family. Instead, the queen assigns the shocked young captain to tutor her out-of-control, tomboy daughter, Marie.

He knows all of the other tutors have failed miserably, and he tries to beg out of it, but the queen will not relent. However, she does give him leave to use any teaching method he likes. Her ultimate command is that she be trained as a lady in preparation for her royal ball.

Angry and humiliated at what he feels is a degrading and impossible assignment, especially for a military captain, he determines to train the princess like he would one of his guardsmen. He will demand strong discipline, tough academics, and sword combat training. He is sure that his rigorous approach will push the princess to complain to her mother, who will then remove him from the assignment.

But to his surprise, Marie instead responds positively to the harsh discipline, and becomes a princess like no other.

And, when they come under attack, her training might be just enough to save both of their lives as they work to unravel who is behind the assassination attempts, and also try to solve the mystery of why the Lord High Chamberlain is such a great sword fighter.

The Mail-Order Bride - http://amzn.com/1480200387

It was to be the big day for Eli. His fiancée, Molly, was coming in on a ship. Two years earlier, unable to find work in England, he had headed for America. His ship was caught in a storm, and he ended up, not in Pennsylvania as he planned, but in Newfoundland.

But that was all behind him now. He had written to Molly every day for the two years, and now she was coming so they could be married.

But Eli was in for a surprise. Unknown to him, Molly had married. She had bought him a mail-order bride, and Eli's life was going to suddenly take an unexpected twist.

About The Author

Daris Howard is an author and playwright who grew up on a farm in rural Idaho. He associated with many colorful characters including cowboys, farmers, lumberjacks and others. Besides his work on the farm he has worked as a cowboy and a mechanic. He was a state champion athlete and competed in college athletics. He also lived for eighteen months in New York.

Daris and his wife, Donna, have ten children and were foster parents for several years. He has also worked in scouting and cub scouts, at one time having 18 boys in his scout troop.

His plays, musicals, and books build on the characters of those he has associated with, along with his many experiences, to bring his work to life.

Daris is a math professor and his classes are well known for the stories he tells to liven up discussion and to help bring across the points he is trying to teach. His scripts and books are much like his stories, full of humor and inspiration.

He and his family have enjoyed running a summer community theatre where he gets a chance to premiere his theatrical works and rework them to make them better. His published plays and books can be seen at http://www.darishoward.com. He has plays translated into German and French and his work has been done in many countries around the world.

In the last few years, Daris has started writing books and short stories. He writes a popular news column called *Life's Outtakes*, that consists of weekly short stories and is published in various newspapers and magazines in the U.S. and Canada including **Country**, **Horizons**, and **Family Living**.

CPSIA information can be obtained
at www.ICGtesting.com
Printed in the USA
LVOW01s1021161215

466834LV00023B/1239/P